CONVERSION
A Spiritual Journey

*Books by Malcolm Muggeridge
available as Fount Paperbacks*

JESUS REDISCOVERED
JESUS — THE MAN WHO LIVES
SOMETHING BEAUTIFUL FOR GOD

available in Fontana

CHRONICLES OF WASTED TIME:

VOL. I THE GREEN STICK
VOL. 2 THE INFERNAL GROVE

CONVERSION

A Spiritual Journey

MALCOLM MUGGERIDGE

COLLINS
8 Grafton Street, London W1
1988

William Collins Sons & Co. Ltd
London · Glasgow · Sydney · Auckland
Toronto · Johannesburg

BRITISH LIBRARY CATALOGUING IN PUBLICATION DATA

Muggeridge, Malcolm
Conversion.
1. Theology, Catholic
I. Title
230'.2   BX1751.2

ISBN 0-00-215144-8

First published 1988
© Malcolm Muggeridge 1988

Photoset in Linotron Sabon by
Rowland Phototypesetting Ltd
Bury St Edmunds, Suffolk
Made and printed in Great Britain by
T. J. Press (Padstow) Ltd, Padstow, Cornwall

I dedicate this book to
LADY COLLINS,
a superb publisher and a dear friend,
to whom I am greatly beholden.

M.M.

CONTENTS

Introduction		11
1	The Child	19
2	Rapture	21
3	The Boy	24
4	The Adolescent	30
5	The Undergraduate	33
6	The Teacher	46
7	The Journalist	59
8	The Soldier	101
9	The Foreign Correspondent	118
10	A Spiritual Pilgrimage	129
11	The Prospect of Death	142
Acknowledgements		151

FOREWORD

God, unto whom all hearts be open, and unto whom all will speaketh, and unto whom no privy thing is hid: I beseech Thee so to cleanse the intent of my heart with the unspeakable gift of Thy grace, that I may perfectly love Thee and worthily praise Thee.

AMEN

The Cloud of Unknowing

God, humble my pride, extinguish the last stirrings of my ego, obliterate whatever remains of worldly ambition and carnality, and in these last days of a mortal existence, help me to serve only Thy purposes, to speak and write only Thy words, to think only Thy thoughts, to have no other prayer than: "Thy will be done." In other words, to be a true Convert.

Introduction

Rite of Reception

The date is 27th November 1982; the place, the Chapel of Our Lady, Help of Christians in the Sussex village of Hurst Green; the occasion, my wife Kitty's and my reception into the Catholic Church. Conducting the ceremony is the Bishop of Arundel, the Rt Rev. Cormac Murphy O'Connor, a tall and kindly man. On one side of him, Father Bidone, an Italian priest belonging to the Order of the Sons of Divine Providence; on the other, the local parish priest, Father Maxwell. (Both, alas, have subsequently died.) All three are robed, the Bishop towering above the other two. I notice with some trepidation that Father Bidone has brought with him some of the mongoloid children cared for in an institution that he was responsible for setting up near Hampton Court. Trepidation because I foresee the children fidgeting, moving about, emitting strange sounds. In fact, when this actually happens, quite unexpectedly and mysteriously a great satisfaction possesses me, transforming what might otherwise be a respectable quiet ceremony into an unforgettable spiritual experience. Afterwards, as I compared notes with Kitty, it turns out that she has had precisely the same experience.

Thinking this over afterwards, I realize that genetic failures are heavenly messengers, with a special role in the world to make outward and visible the physical and mental distortions which we all have inwardly and invisibly. Without dwarfs, we should suppose that all humans were giants, and vice versa. In simpler societies than ours the imperfect specimens – the idiot, the blind, the lame and the dumb – are revered; we call them "handicapped", and persuade ourselves that by murdering them all before or just after they are born, the norm, the model ad-man with his ever-lasting smile exposing his perfect teeth, will become Every-man. Thus the presence and restlessness and strange noises and antics of Father Bidone's children enhances rather than interrupts Kitty's and my reception into the Catholic Church; the most perfect choir singing the most beautiful sacred music could not have done this better. Similarly, Mother Teresa will not allow the ferocious noises of a Calcutta street to be kept out of the chapel where she and her Sisters of Charity worship; at their prayers and receiving the Blessed Sacrament, they must still be reminded of the world, to those poorest of the poor to whom they have dedicated their lives and love.

The service begins with the Bishop delivering his Homily – a word greatly to be preferred to "sermon", of which one has many sad and sometimes ribald memories. In his Homily, the Bishop is kind enough to mention the large number of Catholics who have been praying for our recep-tion into their Church. This, regrettably, stirs up my ego – like a cobra, always ready in all circumstances to lift its head and push out its vicious tongue. I reflect that on high they must have wearied of such persistent appeals – as it might be a lobbyist's over-kill on Capitol Hill in Washing-ton, DC.

After the Homily, Kitty and I step forward with our sponsors, Elizabeth and Frank Longford respectively, dear friends and neighbours.

"Of your own free will," the Bishop says, "you have asked to be received into full communion with the Catholic Church. You have made your decision after careful thought under the guidance of the Holy Spirit. I now invite you to come forward with your sponsor and profess the Catholic faith in the presence of this community. This is the faith in which, for the first time, you will be one with us at the eucharistic table of the Lord Jesus, the sign of the Church's unity."

There follows the Nicene Creed; then, with the Bishop's hand, first on Kitty's head and then on mine, he confirms our entry into the Church, which is sealed with the Gift of the Holy Spirit when he dips his right thumb in the chrism and makes the sign of the cross on our foreheads. Thus our entry into the Church is settled, which gives me, not so much exhilaration as a deep peace; to quote my own words:

> A sense of homecoming, of picking up the threads of a lost life, of responding to a bell that had long been ringing, of taking a place at a table that had long been vacant.

Was it a Conversion?

Being thus received belatedly into the Catholic Church is seen as a conversion, and the hundreds of letters, for the most part loving and congratulatory, that came to Kitty and me, from all over the world, and from all sorts and conditions of people, treat it as such. The same thing happened – though not producing so many letters – when I first became known as an aspiring Christian believer without any denominational tag. This has been at times embarrassing; especially at Evangelical gatherings, when one is liable to be asked precisely how, and in what circumstances, one became a Christian. What is expected is a dramatic account of being converted; something that in the United States became so popular that at one point it almost seemed as though more sinners were being born again than babies being born into the world. The more lurid the old adam, the more impressive the new, so that, in testifying, converts have a way of dwelling upon their past sins and misdemeanours in such detail and so ardently that an element of exhibitionism and even spiritual pornography – if there is such a thing – is liable to creep in.

In my own case, conversion has been more a series of happenings than one single dramatic one. I have a vivid memory of occasions of enlightenment so sharp that they brought a new and lasting dimension of faith into my life. For instance, at Lourdes when I went there to do the commentary for a TV programme. I had expected to be depressed and sceptical about the whole scene; actually, I was greatly uplifted by the courage and cheerfulness of the sick and maimed, and by the loving care accorded them by the helpers and stretcher-bearers. One particular incident has stayed with me. A message was brought to me that a young woman who was dying had said she would like me to visit her. Of course I agreed, and her sister took me to her bedside. She was feverish and emaciated; at first glance, a forbidding sight. Then I noticed her eyes – huge and glowing, and so incredibly beautiful that I was entranced by them. Whereupon all my embarrassment disappeared; all my searching about in my mind for some appropriate sanctimony, became unnecessary. "What beautiful eyes!" I heard myself saying to her sister. She agreed that they were beautiful; her sister, she said, had always had beautiful, glowing eyes. A silence fell upon us, and we were all three caught up in a wonderful joy. I knew, of course, what it was – God's love enfolding us like lights from heaven.

Again, there was a happening when we were in Calcutta with Mother Teresa making the film *Something Beautiful for God*, that might well have provided an occasion for a conversion. The Home for Dying Destitutes where Mother Teresa's Missionaries of Charity take down-and-outs from the streets of Calcutta, was formerly a Hindu temple, and has very poor lighting; so poor that our cameraman, Ken Macmillan, said it would be quite hopeless to film there. However, he was persuaded to take a few inside shots, covering himself with some outside ones that could be used if the others were unusable. When the film came to be processed, the inside shots were bathed in a wonderful soft light, which, as Ken Macmillan agreed, could not be accounted for in earthly terms. Yet there it is, in the film, and in the stills taken from the film. I have no doubt whatever as to what the explanation is: holiness, an expression of love, is luminous; hence the haloes in medieval portraits of saints. The camera had caught this luminosity, without which the film would have come out quite black, as Ken Macmillan proved to himself when he used the same stock in similar circumstances and got no picture at all.

Mother Teresa is, in herself, a living conversion; it is impossible to be with her, to listen to her, to observe what she is doing and how she is doing it, without being in some degree converted. Her total dedication to Christ, her insistence that all our fellow human beings must be treated and helped and loved as though they were Christ, her simple presentation of the Gospel and joy in receiving the sacraments, is quite irresistible. There is no book I've ever read, or discourse I've ever heard, or service I've ever attended, no human relationship or transcendental experience, that has brought me nearer to Christ, or made me more aware of what the Incarnation signifies for us and requires of us.

What, then, is a conversion? The question is like asking "What is falling in love?" There is no standard procedure, no fixed time. Some, like the Apostle Paul, have Damascus Road experiences; I have often myself prayed for such a dramatic happening in my life that would, as it were, start me off on a new calendar, like from B.C. to A.D., and provide a watershed between carnal and spiritual love. Jesus's own image of a conversion is made clear in His conversation with Nicodemus, when he came to see Jesus by night – being born again. No such experience has been vouchsafed me; I have just stumbled on, like Bunyan's Pilgrim, falling into the Slough of Despond, locked up in Doubting Castle, terrified at passing through the Valley of the Shadow of Death; from time to time, by God's mercy, relieved of my burden of sin, but only, alas, soon to acquire it again.

*   *   *

In the early part of my life I used to think of myself as becoming a great writer whose works would figure in the Eng. Lit. textbooks – a Thomas Hardy, a Bernard Shaw, a Marcel Proust. Or as a great orator whose words would hold huge audiences spellbound – a Lloyd George, a Winston Churchill, a Ramsay MacDonald before incoherence set in. Or as a great revolutionary who, in the words of the Magnificat, would "put down the mighty from their seats and exalt the humble and meek" – a Lenin, a Garibaldi, a Gandhi. Even as a great lover before whom beautiful women would fall prostrate in adoration – a Casanova, a Byron, even a Frank Harris. Never for an instant would I have envisaged humbly seeking admission to the most ancient, and – as I considered then – the most doctrinally dubious of all the contemporary churches, with the murkiest record.

Yet it is also true that from my earliest years there was something else going on inside me than vague aspirations to make a name for myself and a stir in the world: something that led me to feel myself a stranger among strangers in a strange land, whose true habitat was elsewhere; that brought an indefinable melancholy into my life, especially in its early years, and, at the same time, a mysterious exaltation, an awareness that, mixed up with the devices and desires of the ego, there were other possibilities and prospects, another destiny whose realization would swallow up time into Eternity, transform flesh into spirit, knowledge into faith and reveal in transcendental terms what our earthly life truly signifies.

This inner, secret life has its own ups and downs, its alternating states of ecstasy and despair. In its ecstatic mood it can flood one's heart and the whole universe with light; in its despairing mood, darken all creation, oneself included. By contrast, all the rest – acquiring money, seducing women, being noticed – the nudge, the whisper: "There he is!" – counts as nothing; no more than stubble burning on a summer's night, racing crackling flames and clouds of smoke, but nothing, nothing. Then the travelling, like Satan in the Book of Job going to and fro in the world and up and down in it; Peking by moonlight, noon in Tokyo, the Taj Mahal in evening twilight, the pyramids at dawn, the Parthenon limelit; all, as Dr Johnson said of the Giant's Causeway, things to see but not to go to see.

Blake writes of a Golden String which we are to pick up and wind into a ball as we go along. If we manage to hold on to it, he tells us, then it will lead us in at Heaven's Gate in Jerusalem's Wall:

> I give you the end of a Golden String,
>   Only wind it into a ball,
> It will lead you in at Heaven's Gate
>   Built in Jerusalem's Wall.

WILLIAM BLAKE

Being received into the Catholic Church is a staging post for me in following this Golden String. From that stance I look back, as John Henry Newman did in his *Apologia Pro Vita Sua*. But what a difference! Newman's history of his religious opinions, as he calls it, is based on superb scholarship, a dedicated life as a priest, first Anglican and then Catholic, sermons of unique clarity and revelation, the works and ways of a saint and a mystic; whereas following my Golden String has led me into noisy newspaper offices and insulated radio and television studios; sent me questing for news in distant and strange places; had me telephoning and writing against the clock, and generalizing from meagre and often non-existent facts. A fantasy scenario at both the transmitting and receiving ends.

I well remember my own first glimpse of Blake's Golden String, glittering in the mud of wilfulness; how I stooped to pick it up, supposing it to be a coin or some golden object, only to find that it was indeed a Golden String, which I thereupon began to wind into a ball. Thenceforth I often lost it, treading it back into the mud wearing dark glasses, losing sight of it for days on end, but always somehow finding it again. I have it still wound into a monstrous ball, though now I am too feeble to carry it far. Even so, I remain confident that before long, with tottering steps, and sweating under its weight, I shall indeed find myself at Jerusalem's Wall with Heaven's Gate built into it.

1

The Child

I begin with a child, myself, some eight decades ago, blue eyes, blond hair, wearing a trilby hat too large for him, belonging to one of his older brothers. He is walking down Broomhall Road in Sanderstead where the family lived in one of the row of semidetached houses. It is a bright summer's afternoon; he is going nowhere in particular, enjoying the feeling of being out on his own without permission, as it might be Tom Sawyer or Huckleberry Finn, two of his heroes. As is his way, he builds up in his mind an imaginary drama: his parents discover his absence, they are distracted. Where can he have gone? What can have befallen him? Then a policeman arrives to break the news to them that their son has been knocked over by a motor car, and is in the General Hospital emergency ward. His parents are rushed there in a police car with the siren sounding, and stand by his bed. He gives them a wan smile, and then closes his eyes expecting to die. Instead, he goes on living.

Having worked this drama out in all its detail, and enacted his own part with gusto, he returns to a consideration of his hat. He is in two minds about it; seeing it, on the one hand, as dashing, and on the other, as absurd. Now, eighty-four years later, he is liable to experience the same mixed feelings over some sartorial or other eccentricity. In the child, too, as in the octogenarian, there is the same recurrent wonderment as to who he is and what he is supposed to be about. As though he had been cued on to the stage only to find that he had forgotten his lines, and anyway rehearsed for a quite different play from the one that was being performed – a lost actor's dream under the spotlight.

In the very first consciousness of childhood there is an awareness of some benign spirit – God – watching over our human condition; as there are also built into the night shapes and shadows and strange awesome sounds. With the passage of time these impressions are liable to get blurred and mistaken for one another. With old age comes what is called second childhood, so that we may meet our Maker precisely as we left Him – as little children who, the Gospels tell us, alone are able to understand what He came into the world to tell us.

> How like an angel came I down!
>   How bright are all things here!
> When first among His works I did appear,
>   Oh, how their Glory me did crown!
> The world resembled His Eternity,
>   In which my soul did walk;
> And everything that I did see
>   Did with me talk.
>
> The skies in their magnificence,
>   The lively, lovely air;
> Oh, how divine, how soft, how sweet, how fair!
>   The stars did entertain my sense,
> And all the work of God so bright and pure,
>   So rich and great did seem
> As if they ever must endure
>   In my esteem.

THOMAS TRAHERNE

2

Rapture

The most characteristic and uplifting of the manifestations of conversion is rapture – an inexpressible joy which suffuses our whole being, making our fears dissolve into nothing, and our expectations all move heavenwards. No earthly image can convey this adequately; music at its best – say, Mozart's *Exultate* – gets nearer to it than words. It is like coming to after an anaesthetic, with lost faces and voices and shapes again becoming recognizable. Or like getting film back into sync, so that the speaking and the pictures sort themselves out and become clear instead of confused. The so-called successes and achievements on which we pride ourselves, and which bring us such inordinate satisfaction, are, indeed, a kind of anaesthetic; emerging from them – Pascal calls them all diversions of one sort and another – we resume contact with reality.

Pascal's own conversion illustrates this. He had been thinking of Peter; of his thrice-repeated denial that he was in any way connected with Jesus, and then the cock crowing and his bitter tears. I have myself found that, reading of this, it is hard to keep back my own tears, so conscious am I of similar betrayals. Pascal, too, wept as he recalled his own disloyalty; and a dreadful desolation came upon him, which then suddenly melted away as he remembered that he, too, could be forgiven. In his methodical way, as though he were documenting one of his scientific experiments, he notes it all down, with the triumphant conclusion:

"Certainty, certainty, joy, peace. God of Jesus Christ. *Deum meum et Deum vostram*. Oblivion of the world and of everything except God." He kept this record always about his person; when he died it was found sewn into his coat.

Then, at the other extreme, the dark night. The light has gone out, no glimmer anywhere, only darkness; no hope of any kind, except for death, not to be, not to exist at all. Even flattery – the fan-letter *in excelsia* – falls like a lustreless kiss on a dead cheek. Heaven or hell a matter of indifference; let there be nothingness, *Fiat nihil!* Throughout nights of sleeplessness and misery, only one longing – for obliteration; likewise when the words will not come, the mind will not think, the pen will not write. And yet, as I am well aware, all this is so much theatre; and the billions upon billions of fellow humans who have lived, are living and will live on our little earth, have only one recourse – to put aside every other consideration, the backwards and the forwards, hope and despair, ardour and listlessness, and get down on their knees to pray with the utmost humility, and utterly meaning it: "Thy will be done", confident that our Creator's purpose for His creation is to do with love rather than power, with peace and not strife, with Eternity rather than Time, and with our souls rather than our bodies or our minds.

Thus in the turmoil of life without, and black despair within, it is always possible to turn aside and wait on God. Just as at the centre of a hurricane there is stillness, and above the clouds a clear sky, so it is possible to make a little clearing in the jungle of our human will for a rendezvous with God. He will always turn up, though in what guise and in what circumstances cannot be foreseen – perhaps trailing clouds of glory, perhaps as a beggar; in the purity of the desert or in the squalor of London's Soho or New York's Times Square. Once, in Times Square, I was glancing disconsolately, but also avidly, at the rows and rows of paperbacks, each with some lewd or sadistic picture for its cover, and noticed that by some strange accident my book on Mother Teresa, *Something Beautiful for God*, had got on to these sad shelves. Wondering how it could have happened, Herbert's beautiful lines came into my mind:

> And here in dust and dirt, O here
> The lilies of His love appear.

For every situation and eventuality there is a parable if you look carefully enough.

3

The Boy

The child last seen walking down Broomhall Road, Sanderstead, in a trilby hat too large for him, and wondering who he is and why, is now a schoolboy at a government elementary school in South Croydon. No blazers or caps in those days at such schools; just classrooms and teachers and an asphalt playground. At the morning assembly there is a hymn and prayers, and scripture is a compulsory subject. The headmaster leads the prayers, taking particular care over the aspirates, especially "Hallowed be Thy name" – tricky one; there are occasions when a repetition of the prayer is called for to get it right. Our Boy follows the attitude towards hymns and prayers at home, and tends to sabotage the morning hymn by singing out of tune (not that he can ever sing in tune), and by devising awkward questions at scripture lessons.

One such question which caused some embarrassment at the time, arises out of the frequent mention in the Bible, New Testament as well as Old, of how this or that had to happen or be said "in order that the prophecy might be fulfilled". How can it be an authentic prophecy, the Boy asks his teacher, if steps have to be taken and words spoken to bring it to pass? His teacher is flummoxed, to the Boy's great satisfaction. In his mind, however, the question continues to germinate. Over the years he comes to see that, assuming God had a purpose in creating our earth and the universe, we, His creatures, have no choice but to fulfil it, knowing that it will be fulfilled anyway. Thus, the universe can be seen as a theatre, Christ as the play, the Bible as the script, and ourselves, mankind, as the actors, all of whom have lines to say and entrances and exits to make. Our free will is our freedom to speak our allotted lines and enact our allotted parts, and God's creation may be compared rather with Shakespeare writing *King Lear*, or Beethoven composing his *Missa Solemnis* or Michelangelo painting the Sistine Chapel, than with planning a garden suburb, preparing a Beveridge Report, setting up a dictatorship of the proletariat, or otherwise planning an earthly paradise. On this reckoning, the Incarnation is God's masterpiece; hence the aptness of "in the beginning was the Word . . ." Not a matter of a big bang or a series of little ones as scientists dispute, no natural, or unnatural, selection; just the Word dwelling among us full of grace and truth.

The teacher to whom the Boy's question is addressed is Helen Corke, only just out of training college, and already acquainted with another Croydon teacher – D. H., or, as she calls him, David, Lawrence. A weekend together in the Isle of Wight was a sort of early rehearsal of subsequent more stormy engagements, with Corke as the first Lady Chatterley. Years later, when Corke had grown into a little white-haired, bent old lady, and the Boy was also white-haired, the two of them were filmed for TV documentary purposes, walking together across the asphalt playground to the tune of "Now the day is over", the liberation hymn sung on Friday afternoons.

At the Boy's home the Christian religion is in abeyance, replaced by the religion of progress, whereby men of good will are preparing to take over, the Boy's father among them. No God, they consider, is needed any longer. He must be considered dead, or at any rate, as in retirement. As for Jesus Christ – He cared for the poor, consorted with publicans and prostitutes, denounced the upper classes of the day, the scribes and Pharisees, fell foul of King Herod and was disrespectful to the Roman Governor, Pontius Pilate. So naturally He was executed by the very inhumane means used by the Romans – crucifixion.

The Boy's ardour is stirred by the prospect of bringing heaven down to earth, and creating here and now a brotherly, peaceful and prosperous society: to each according to his needs, from each according to his capacity. At outdoor meetings the blueprint for such a society is expounded by his father and echoed by the son, who very early on, when in his teens, experiences the excitement of public speaking; of stirring an audience up – like giving hunting hounds a scent to follow, or whores dressed up and making obscene gestures to excite prospective clients. "Give us your votes," we seemed to be saying, "and we will give you your happiness – schools and universities to educate you, houses fit for you to live in, hospitals to heal you, liberation from your present servitude to exacting and callous masters. You yourselves to become the masters – owning the mines and factories you work in, the trams and trains you drive, the Co-op shops where you spend your money and collect your divi. You yourselves the bosses, the lords of creation, with no God to pray to, or employers to kowtow to; in charge of your own lives and your own destiny – if only you will vote for us."

On a Saturday evening, standing on a gimcrack platform at the corner of Surrey Street where there is an open-air market lit by flares, such words go to the Boy's head. What a wonderful prospect after the slaughter and destruction of the 1914–18 war! Now, thanks to the newly established League of Nations, nothing of the kind will ever occur again; it was truly a war to end war, so that we shall live at peace for evermore.

In this splendid scenario there is no place for a God or need for a Saviour – something that even then for some mysterious reason shakes the Boy's certainty. Would the Children of Israel, he wonders, ever have found their way across the wilderness to the Promised Land without the pillar of fire to guide them? Can the great drama of the Incarnation be just a fairy tale or fable, and the central character be just a good and public-spirited man – as it were, the Honourable Member for Galilee South in the Labour interest? Even before he had the slightest notion as to what it signified, the Boy is caught up in the New Testament story, as though it were somehow burnt into him, and he has always known it. The birth in Bethlehem, the shepherds and the Magi with their gifts, the Mother feeding her child, born out of wedlock and into Eternity; every detail, as though in some previous existence he had been a participant. It was something he was to learn – that the most profound truths are characterized by seeming, once recognized, to have been always known, and the most profound love, once experienced, to have always existed, so that you see a face and hear a voice familiar from the beginning of time, and always to be familiar – every truth an echo, every love without a beginning or an end.

An idea becomes close to you only when you are aware of it in your soul, when in reading about it it seems to you that it has already occurred to you, that you know it and are simply recalling it. That's how it was when the Boy read the Gospels. In the Gospels he discovered a new world; he had not supposed that there was such depth of thought in them. Yet it all seemed so familiar; it seemed he had known it all long ago, that he had only forgotten it.

Truth can never be told so as to be understood, and not be believed, Tolstoy said, as recorded in Bulgakov's Diary, 18th April 1910.

Everything possible to be believed is an image of truth.

BLAKE

Scripture as such plays a negligible role in the Boy's up-bringing. Corke is not prone to it, though she herself came from a biblical home; the headmaster fulfils only the minimum requirements of the latest Education Act, and at the Boy's home the Bible is seldom opened, and then usually to check some ironical quote from it. The only exception is when the Boy's maternal grandmother is visiting them. She comes from Sheffield, has brought up a large family on the wages of a factory-worker, and has her wits about her. Once when the Boy is trying to be funny about Daniel in the lions' den, she turns on him and says: "If Daniel isn't true, nothing is!" This saying echoes in his mind as a valid statement. If, say, Darwin's theory of evolution isn't true, no matter. What is it but a far-fetched exercise in theorizing and credulity that may well amuse posterity for generations to come? But if the Bible were to be subtracted from what we continue to call Western Civilization, or Christendom, it would leave a great hole in our *mores*, in our art and literature, music and architecture; in our culture altogether, besides depriving us of the faith whereby, with much backsliding, much erring and stray-ing like lost sheep, we have lived through the Christian centuries.

The Boy acquires a Bible of his own and reads it surrep-titiously, as it might have been some forbidden book like *Fanny Hill*. He puts a brown paper cover on it so that no one will know what particular book he is reading; he marks passages, and, strangest of all, he takes it to bed with him, opened at some passage that has particularly impressed and moved him, as though it will protect and comfort him through the night hours when, as often happens – and has continued to happen at all stages in his life – he is sleepless, turning over and over in his mind some dilemma or fear while on edge at the strange sounds the night holds. Years later he comes across this Bible among his books, and notes how crumpled and torn it is, and how the worst ravages are in the passages relating to the Passion – there, stains that might be from tears.

The Adolescent

The Boy now moves into adolescence and becomes aware of sexuality; having the good fortune to miss out on what has come to be called "sex education", he has only the vaguest notion of what this signifies. In his mutilated Bible he underscores a sentence in the eighth chapter of the Epistle to the Romans: "For to be carnally minded is death, but to be spiritually minded is life and peace." And another in the fifth chapter of the Epistle to the Galatians: "For the flesh lusteth against the spirit and the spirit against the flesh; and these are contrary, the one to the other, so that ye cannot do the things that ye would." These two sentences haunt him over the years even though he constantly fails to act upon them, easily and often engaging in what Pascal calls "licking the earth".

He falls in love, but lust intrudes; he follows lust, and love intrudes. It is the beginning of a long struggle, with many ups and downs, horrors and ersatz ecstasy, broken promises and betrayals. As for truth, it gets lost in the quicksands of history, the jungle of facts, the slough of the consensus, and finally the computer swallows it up.

The war ends, to the Boy's chagrin; he had hoped that it would go on long enough for him to become a participant, but misses this by a year. From the top of a bus he observes with wonder the Armistice Day celebrations – a sort of victory debauchery ushering in the era of permissiveness. Later, in Berlin, he sees the corresponding debauchery of

defeat, glamourized in the writings of Christopher Isher-
wood. As things turn out, the prophet, or guru, of this
world fit for libertines to live in proves to be none other
than Corke's boyfriend, D. H. Lawrence. Long afterwards,
when the Boy has become a grown-up man, thumbing over
the pages of a picture book, *D. H. Lawrence and his
World*, he comes upon the reproduction of a painting by
Collingwood Gee of Lawrence reading *Lady Chatterley's
Lover* to Reginald Turner, Norman Douglas and Pino
Orioli in Orioli's house in Florence. Surely, he muses, there
must be some link between these three listeners; then the
penny drops, they are the three leading pederasts of Europe.
So, what Blake calls Fearful Symmetry reveals itself; a
dying, impotent man launches what is to become the most
famous contemporary celebration of human sexuality to
an audience of three eminent homosexuals. Truly God is
not mocked.

As the Boy grows into manhood these inner meanings,
essays in Fearful Symmetry, become a major preoccupation.
He comes to see that all happenings down to the tiniest
gesture, all words however casually spoken, every thought
and speculation, looked at with eyes that see and listened
to with ears that hear, are conveying something; as it might
be in cipher. To crack the cipher a code book is necessary;
the Gospels and the Epistles in the New Testament provide
it. Thus can be seen, underlying the chaos of the world and
of a spectator's own mind, God's order. Nature itself is
speaking to us, if we can only hear it, of His purposes for
His creatures and creation. As for history, billed as an
interminably running soap opera, it turns out on closer
inspection to be a Theatre of Fearful Symmetry.

I understand these passages (from Clement of Alexan-
dria and Origen) to mean that the exterior world,
physical and historical, was but the manifestation of

our sense of realities greater than itself. Nature was a parable, scripture was an allegory; pagan literature, philosophy, and mythology, properly understood, were but a preparation for the Gospel . . . The visible world still remains without its divine interpretation. Holy Church in her sacraments will remain even to the end of the world after all but a symbol of those heavenly facts which will fill eternity. Her mysteries are but the expressions in human language of truths to which the human mind is unequal . . . Christianity itself is a living idea, which, as time goes on, enters upon strange territory. Points of controversy alter its bearing; parties rise and fall around it; dangers and hopes appear in new relations, and old principles reappear under new forms. *It changes with them in order to remain the same* . . . The human mind in its present state is unequal to its own powers of appreciation; *it embraces more than it can master* . . . A religious mind is ever looking out of itself, is ever recalling to itself Him on whom it depends, and who is the centre of all truth and good . . . The dividing line between God and the world goes through each man's heart. The worldly man is one whose heart is so earthbound that he has forgotten that he is made for heaven . . . The sinner would not enjoy heaven if he went there; not till he has turned from his sin and is once more looking towards God.

JOHN HENRY NEWMAN

The Undergraduate

The schoolboy now becomes the Undergraduate; the scene shifts from Croydon to Cambridge, where for the first time he comes into intimate contact with clergymen, actual and aspiring, and attends regular chapel services – at Selwyn College compulsory. Is this a conversion? In a sense, yes, in that it involves some sort of Christian life as distinct from belief. He has always been given to praying; not just kneeling down at a particular time and in particular circumstances, but inwardly crying for mercy, for help – "Save me! Guide me! Use me!" Now he becomes familiar with the Book of Common Prayer, that liturgical master-piece; with the order of services – Matins, Evensong, even the Litany which counts as a full service but is substantially shorter than the regular ones. Also he weaves into his life penitential offerings – that he has erred and strayed from God's ways like a lost sheep, followed too much the devices and desires of his own heart, left undone those things that he ought to have done and done those things he ought not to have done. His favourite prayer becomes, and remains, St Chrysostom's: that his desires and petitions may be fulfilled "as may be most expedient" for him. The Eucharist, too, comes to have a special significance; he sips the wine and munches the wafer, longing to taste them as the blood and body of Christ, and consequently to walk back to his seat in the congregation in a kind of trance. But this does not happen; he is as wide awake on his return journey from the altar rail as on making his way to it, there to kneel and receive the sacraments. Sometimes he simulates the trance in the hope that thereby it might authentically come to pass, but it doesn't.

As for God Himself, in those far-off days undergraduates were required to take an examination in Divinity – known as "divvers" – which involved studying Paley's *Evidences of Christianity*, first published in 1704, and purporting to prove, among other things, God's existence. Our student manages to master the *Evidences* to the point of satisfying the examiner, but in thus "proving" God's existence, he finds that actually it has been called in question. In the same sort of way, when one of the Soviet astronauts proudly announced that in the stratosphere he had found no trace of Heaven, he was, had he but known it, supporting, not denying, Heaven's existence; a trace of Heaven on his radar-screen would have undermined belief in it for years to come.

To look for God, Pascal tells us, is to find Him, and having found Him, we can never again be permanently separated. We may lose contact with Him for long periods of time, drowning ourselves in our own carnality and exalting ourselves in our own pride; we may even in our madness curse His name, ridicule His worship and manifestations, confute Him with notions of Man's self-propelling ascent from primeval slime to *homo sapiens*, and go so far as to announce His decease, and even, with insane pride, claim to have murdered Him. Yet still at the end of the day there is nothing for it but to fall on to our knees and pray, meaning it utterly, "Thy will be done!", in the knowledge that God's purpose for us is a loving and creative one, and that in fulfilling it we are participants in His love and care for His creation.

Thus bemused, the Undergraduate finds himself for the first time in his life looking round desperately for help, and in so doing the word "Faith" comes into his mind. How can it be attained?, he asks himself. What is it? Certainly not, as many of his coevals appear to believe, merely a device for believing what is unbelievable, and deriving comfort from imaginary or false premises. Rather, as he has read in the Epistle to the Hebrews, "Faith is the substance of things hoped for, the evidence of things not seen." In other words, Faith is a special kind of knowledge, as the process for acquiring it is a special kind of education. Though we have to accept the impenetrability of the Cloud of Unknowing that lies between us in Time and the Eternity that is our true habitat, Faith provides a special insight into the mystery that lies at the heart of our earthly existence. We cannot resolve the mystery, but seeing it as a parable, and scripture expounding it as an allegory, we can make guesses at what it signifies. And what inspired guesses there have been! Chartres Cathedral, for one – what a guess that was! And Shakespeare's *King Lear*, and the Book of Job, Milton's *Paradise Lost* and Dante's *Divine Comedy* and the Sistine Chapel, Pascal's *Pensées* and Blake's *Songs of Innocence* and *Songs of Experience* and Beethoven's *Missa Solemnis*. Indeed, every true word ever uttered, every thought sincerely and lucidly entertained, every harmonious note sung or sounded, laughter flashing like lightning between the head and the heart, human love in all its diversity binding together husbands and wives, parents and children, grandparents and grandchildren, and making of all mankind one family and our earth their home; the earth itself with its colours and shapes and smells, and its setting in a universe growing ever vaster and its basic components becoming ever more microscopic – seen with the eyes of Faith, it all adds up to a oneness, an image of everlasting reality.

Of course, it goes without saying that, when at last we pass through the Cloud of Unknowing and the mystery is unravelled, all the preceding guesswork will seem by comparison with what is then revealed as no more than the scribble of children before they have learned their letters. To prepare us for that ultimate enlightenment, and to encourage us meanwhile to endure our human condition, we have been accorded the great mercy of the Incarnation which Faith enables us to see as a drama; in its totality, a full and perfect expression of all the hopes our mouths cannot utter, and all the convictions our minds cannot formulate. To approach this great drama of the Incarnation as history is like, say, measuring Shakespeare's Caesar against Plutarch's; to take it into the laboratory to be tested is as absurd as looking in a blown-up photograph of a sunrise for Blake's vision of the dawn as angels climbing up and down a ladder between Heaven and Earth. Confronted with the Incarnation, God is brought within the range of our understanding; God Himself becomes His own parable, which Faith, in wonder and humility, can elucidate.

> Such is Faith, springing up out of the immortal seed of love, and ever budding forth in new blossoms and maturing new fruit ... constraining the reason to accept mysteries, the hand to work, the feet to run, the voice to bear witness as the case may be, these acts ... arising from Faith seeing the invisible world, and love choosing it.
>
> JOHN HENRY NEWMAN

Jean-Pierre de Caussade insisted that:

> Faith is the light of time, it alone recognizes truth without seeing it, touches what it cannot feel, looks upon this world as though it did not exist, sees what is not apparent. It is the key to celestial treasures, the key to the unfathomable mystery and knowledge of God. Faith conquers all the fantasy of falsehood;

through faith God reveals and manifests Himself, defying all things. Faith removes the veil and uncovers eternal truth. When souls are given the understanding of faith, God speaks to them through all creation, and the universe becomes for them a living testimony which the finger of God continually traces before their eyes, the record of every passing moment, a sacred scripture. The sacred books which the Holy Spirit has dictated are only the beginnings of divine guidance for us. Everything that happens is a continuation of the scriptures, expounding for us what has not been written. Faith explains the one through the other. It is an abstraction presenting the vast extent of divine action summarized in the scriptures, in which souls can discover the key to all its mysteries . . . Faith is only living at its best when sensible appearances contradict and attempt to destroy it . . . To find God is good in the trivial and most ordinary events as in the greatest; is to have not an ordinary, but a great and extraordinary faith . . . How delightful the peace one enjoys when one has learned by faith to see God in this way through all creatures as through a transparent veil. Darkness becomes light and bitterness sweet . . . There is nothing that faith does not penetrate and seek out. It passes beyond darkness, and no matter how deep the shadows, it passes through them to the truth which it always finally embraces, and from which it is never separated.

At Selwyn College the prevailing style is Anglo-Catholic, with a propensity to call all clergymen "Father", burn incense, wear birettas and generally emulate the Roman rite. Many of the ordinands are ex-servicemen, lately in the trenches, who still sport their British Warms, and try to impersonate Woodbine Willie, Tubby Clayton, and other famous wartime padres. Of the Anglo-Catholic ordinands, the one who impresses the Undergraduate most is Alec Vidler, in his fourth year and soon to be ordained, good at games, with a First in his Theology Tripos, and altogether an outstanding figure in the college. To the Undergraduate's great surprise and delight, the two of them become friends despite the gap between them in years, in scholarship, in games and in their standing in the college – a friendship that is to last all their lives, so that they find themselves still friends and near neighbours as Octogenarians.

His friendship with Vidler and acquaintance with the circle of Anglo-Catholics in which he moves, brings the Undergraduate into contact with the Church, not just as a holy and sometimes absurd relic of the past, but as a living and continuing manifestation of the Holy Spirit. Kneeling before the reserved Sacrament, he prays long and earnestly for a sign – some vision or emanation that will give him a foretaste of the life of Eternity lying ahead. But nothing happens; he is vouchsafed no such sign, and has to reconcile himself to searching for the supernatural in nature and for Eternity in Time. Through his friendship with Vidler the Undergraduate gets into the way of visiting Oratory house, headquarters of the Anglican Order of the Good Shepherd, consisting of ordained clergy who go out to the parishes or other priestly duties while at the same time fulfilling the vows they have taken – the classic ones of chastity, poverty and obedience – and every so often meet together in a retreat. For two terms of the Undergraduate's time at Cambridge, he stays at Oratory house; a period of great, and, for him, unusual contentment, when the days pass smoothly, broken up by the daily offices and certain duties. These include such things as serving at the morning Euchar-ist, ringing the Angelus, working in the garden with Father Wilfred Knox, a saintly man, one of four famous brothers, the other three being Evoe, an editor of *Punch*; Ronnie, a

Catholic convert and accomplished versifier and don; and Dilly, a cipher-cracker of high repute in both the 1914–18 and the 1939–45 wars.

The Undergraduate's sense of well-being at Oratory House, and edification at the offices and services in the little chapel, makes him wonder whether he may not have a vocation for the religious life. Certainly, then and subsequently, he finds that abstemious ways make for happiness, and self-indulgence, especially sexual, for misery and remorse. To put aside worldly ambition, lechery, the ego's clamorous demands, what joy! To succumb, what misery!

Tuning of my Breast

Yet take Thy way, for sure Thy way is best:
Stretch or contract me, Thy poor debtor:
This is but tuning of my breast,
To make the music better.

GEORGE HERBERT

Suddenly, unaccountably, joy, peace, illumination, total submersion in God's universal love, come to the Undergraduate and he sits or moves about in ecstasy. If he looks out of the window, it is to see paradise; if he is with other human beings, they are angels; if he closes his eyes and meditates, he floats away from his physical existence and desires, from his very prayers and devotions, and finds himself near to some ineffable, ultimate truth, breathing the very perfume of God's love and loitering in the very precincts of Heaven, so that as its gates swing open and shut he hears gusts of celestial music and celestial laughter.

* * *

It is not unusual for living suddenly to lose all its savour. Bunyan, Tolstoy, Muhammad, Wesley and innumerable others passed through this mood. In each case, the mood was the same – all the things that are supposed to give delight (money, sensuality, success, etc.) lose their savour, becoming pointless, utterly futile. Then comes the thirst for eternity. Oh, this terrible thirst! Nothing will satisfy except what is unattainable. "God!" they cry out, or: "Woe!", and long for solitude. In solitude Eternity is a little less remote than amidst the distractions of the world. Perhaps they break in the struggle, and then are more utterly lost than before. If they come through the struggle they are listened to; their voices demand and get a hearing. This puts power within their grasp. Christ died to escape power, Muhammad lived to wield it. Power is the greatest snare of all. How terrible is power in all its manifestations – the voice raised to command, the hand stretched out to seize, the eyes burning with appetite. Money had better be given away; organizations had better be disbanded; bodies had better lie separately. I climbed on to another body howling out passion, and then lay still longing for God; like a soldier exhausted with the battle, resting, but only to get up again and continue fighting. There is no peace at all, except in looking across Time at Eternity beyond – as one looks at a distant view from a mountain top.

Now a strange thing! Despite the Undergraduate's showing off propensity, the masquerade of his daily life, he is fitfully aware of some stupendous reality; some overwhelming truth which encompasses all the trivialities of opinion and argument; a great light that swallows up the darkness and the little human candles that ornament it. So, licking the earth, he is transported into the sky; instead of just celebrating the Incarnation, rejoicing over the birth and resurrection of the central figure – Jesus – and the mourning over His brutal death, he is a participant. As such, he fully realizes for the first time that God, by becoming a man, truly reaches down to men so that they might the better relate themselves to Him. Also, that the Cross, in itself a gallows, an object of horror, because of its role in the Incarnation becomes a symbol of everything that is most fulfilling and most creative in human life. Taken by the Apostle Paul to a dissolving Roman Empire, the Cross ushers in Christendom's two thousand years; clutched in dying hands, it makes death beautiful; as Pastor Bonhoeffer put it, a beginning rather than an end, which teaches all of us who have eyes to see and ears to hear that in suffering we learn and live, whereas if suffering were to be eliminated from the experience of living, as some twentieth-century minds have considered possible, far from thereby enhancing our mortal existence, it would become futile and unbearable.

What appealed to him were the wild extravagances of Faith; the New Testament phrases about God's wisdom being men's foolishness, St Francis of Assisi rejoicing at being naked on the naked earth, Blake's strange vision of the *Marriage of Heaven and Hell.* Surveying the abysmal chasm between his certainty that everything human beings tried to achieve was inadequate to the point of being farcical, that mortality itself was a kind of gargoyle joke, and his equal certainty that every moment of every day was full of enchantment and infinitely precious, that human love was the nearest image vouchsafed us of God's love irradiating the whole universe; that, indeed, embedded in each grain of sand, there is veritably a world, to be explored, as geologists explore the antiquity of fossils through their markings, and astronauts through their flights into outer space – surveying this chasm, yawning in its vastness to the point of inducing total insanity, tearing us into schizophrenic pieces, he grasped that over it lay, as it were, a cable-bridge, frail, swaying, but passable. And this bridge, this reconciliation between the black despair of lying bound and gagged in the tiny dungeon of the ego, and soaring upwards into the white radiance of God's universal love –

this bridge was the Incarnation, whose truth expresses that of the desperate needs it meets.

* * *

Because of our physical hunger, we know there is bread; because of our spiritual hunger, we know there is Christ.

> The most godly knowing of God is that which is known by unknowing . . . For once men thought it meekness to say naught of their own heads, unless they confirmed it by Scripture and doctor's words, and now it is turned into curiosity and display of knowledge . . . This naught and this nowhere are nothing else than the divine Cloud of Unknowing . . . Let be this everywhere and this aught, in comparison of this nowhere and this naught . . . imagination is a power through the which we portray all images of all absent and present things; and both it and the thing that it worketh in be contained in the mind. Before Man sinned, was imagination so obedient unto the reason – to that which it is as it were servant – that it ministered never to any disordered image of any bodily creature; and now it is not so. For unless it be restrained by the light of grace in the reason, it will never cease, sleeping or waking, to portray diverse disordered images of bodily creatures; or else some fantasy, the which is naught else but a bodily conceit of a ghostly thing, or else a ghostly conceit of a bodily thing. And this is evermore feigned and false, and next unto error.
>
> *Cloud of Unknowing*

The Undergraduate keeps his secret spiritual life to himself, and ostensibly falls in with the prevailing postwar mood of mild debauchery. Occasionally becoming tipsy, boasting of imaginary amorous adventures, getting into debt, grumbling over compulsory chapel attendance, attempting with little success to play games, and neglecting his studies – a Natural Science Tripos comprehending physics, chemistry and zoology, which anyway has little interest for him. In retrospect, all he can remember of it is dissecting a dogfish, though to what end remains wrapped in mystery. None the less, he somehow manages to rustle up a pass degree; in those days to fail altogether was almost impossible.

Despite the desultory nature of his studies, they serve to give the Undergraduate a vague awareness of Science as a kind of rival ersatz religion to Christianity, now firmly entrenched in the whole structure of contemporary learning and technology – A Christian Science, in its pretensions reaching far beyond anything Mary Baker Eddy had in mind. Thus, for instance, out of the theory of Darwinian evolution comes the whole notion of social progress; just as, through the operation of Natural Selection, the most primitive forms of life are seen as progressing to the most sophisticated, primeval slime becoming Bertrand Russell, thereby creating a climate of Utopian hopes, which, however, carry within themselves the seeds of their own dissolution.

Pascal, one of the most brilliant scientific minds of his time, came to realize that, as a pursuit, science is a cul-de-sac, and results in the dethronement of God and the elevation of men, to the point that they come to see themselves as lords of creation – a role that either makes them go quite mad, or sink into mere animality. Blake, too, in his own bizarre way, saw that the so-called Enlightenment was in truth a darkening of the spirit, and scrawled across his copy of Bacon's *Essays* – a fore-runner of Huxley's – "Good Advice for Satan's Kingdom". Likewise, in some dim way the Undergraduate feels utterly disillusioned with the scientific books, lectures and laboratory sessions he has so neglected; and when quite casually an Evangelical clergyman with a kindly, open face offers him a teaching post at

a lately founded Christian college in South India, he closes
with the offer then and there.

> It is in vain, O men, that you seek within yourselves the
> cure of all your miseries. All your insight only leads you
> to the knowledge that it is not in yourselves that you
> will discover the true and the good. The philosophers
> promised them to you, and have not been able to keep
> their promise . . . Your principal maladies are pride,
> which cuts you off from God; sensuality, which binds
> you to the earth; and they have done nothing but foster
> at least one of these maladies. If they have given you
> God for your object, it has only been to pander to your
> pride; they made you think that you were like Him and
> resembled Him by your nature. And those who have
> grasped the vanity of such a pretension have cast you
> down into the other abyss by making you believe that
> your nature was like that of the beasts of the field, and
> have led you to seek your good in lust, which is the lot
> of animals.   PASCAL

> In our day, everything that is most retrograde in the
> spirit of religion has taken refuge, above all, in science
> itself. A science like ours, essentially closed to the
> layman, and therefore to scientists themselves – be-
> cause each of them is a layman outside his own narrow
> specialization – is the proper theology of an ever
> increasingly bureaucratic society. "It is secrecy, mys-
> tery, that is everywhere the soul of bureaucracy",
> wrote Marx in his youth; and mystery is founded upon
> specialization. Mystery is the condition of all privilege
> and consequently of all oppression; and it is in science
> itself, the breaker of idols, the destroyer of mystery,
> that mystery has found its last refuge.
>   SIMONE WEIL

Mock on, Mock on Voltaire, Rousseau:
Mock on, Mock on; 'tis all in vain!
You throw the sand against the wind,
And the wind blows it back again.

BLAKE

Before leaving Cambridge the Undergraduate – now a
Graduate of sorts – makes the acquaintance of Kitty Dobbs,
the sister of a fellow undergraduate with whom he shared
rooms for a time. It proved to be one of those fateful
encounters belonging to Always rather than Now. After
meeting Kitty he cannot imagine a time when he did not
know her, and equally, from that moment, cannot envisage
any future without her. Such is love in its true dimension
– a knot in Blake's Golden String; a reminder that, though
sojourners in Time, Eternity is our true habitat.

But as all several souls contain
   Mixture of things they know not what,
Love these mix'd souls doth mix again,
   And makes both one, each this, and that.
A single violet transplant,
   The strength, the colour, and the size –
All which before was poor and scant –
   Redoubles still and multiplies.
When love with one another so
   Interanimates two souls
That abler soul, which thence doth flow,
   Defects of loneliness controls.
We, then, who are this new soul, know,
   Of what we are composed, and made,
For th'atomies of which we grow
   Are souls, whom no change can invade.

JOHN DONNE

6

The Teacher

In December 1924, the Teacher takes a P. & O. boat to Colombo in Ceylon – now Sri Lanka – and from there makes his way to Alwaye, in what was then the Indian state of Travancore – now Kerala. His fellow passengers seem a friendly, cheerful lot, but as the voyage proceeds he notices that they become somehow more deliberate; their voices as they order a drink in the bar are more authoritative. Instead of shouting, "Waiter!", they shout, "Boy!", irrespective of the waiter's years. By the time they reach the Suez Canal and the weather gets warmer, the solar topees, or pith helmets, are brought out; the men put on their white suits, and the ladies their summer dresses and unfold their sunshades – all symptoms of the Raj manifesting itself as the ship approaches India. The topees, considered essential headgear in the Indian sun, are the hallmark of the authentic Sahib. When, some twenty-five years hence, the Raj comes to an end, they disappear with it almost overnight.

By this time the Teacher is definitely a grown man who smokes a pipe and eyes females lasciviously. On the ship, his social position under the Raj is somewhat anomalous; he has the requisite credentials to be regarded as a Sahib, but he is sharing his cabin with an Indian clergyman from Travancore, the Rev. C. K. Jacob – a situation which, as the Raj manifests itself, is seen by most of the passengers as "all wrong", and as putting the Teacher in the position of a missionary, or "poor white", as distinct from an authentic Sahib, whether some sort of government official or box-wallah – i.e. business man. From the Teacher's point of view, the only disagreeable consequence of sharing a cabin with the Rev. C. K. Jacob is that he feels bound to sit next to him in the dining saloon and to walk up and down the deck with him in case he should feel ostracized, and, truth to tell, his company in large doses proves some-what tedious. He is, in fact, through no fault of his own, a kind of parody or understudy of an old-style conventional clergyman. In the same sort of way, as the Teacher learns susbsequently, Indian army officers are parodies of the Sandhurst model, and students and dons at Indian univer-sities parodies of their Oxford and Cambridge prototypes. The worst consequence of Imperialism or Colonialism, the Teacher comes to realize, is that subject people tend to copy their masters. No doubt the ancient Britons wore hand-made, ill-fitting togas, and drove rickety chariots furiously whenever they had a chance.

The Teacher becomes even more aware of this relation-ship between a subject people and their masters on the last part of his journey by train, bus and steamboat from Colombo to Alwaye, when he finds himself an authentic Sahib by virtue of having parted from the Rev. C. K. Jacob. Being white and English, and consequently the recipient of the respect and attention that went therewith, he found, for instance, queues dissolving before him, seats being provided for him, and other such small favours. At the Union Christian College itself he is more a subject of curiosity than of subservience. As time passes he comes to be taken for granted, the more so because he soon takes to wearing Indian dress – a shirt and dhoti made of *kadi*, homespun cloth, and the uniform of followers of Gandhi. Despite this gesture, he is still a Sahib, if an informal one. He belongs to the Raj, not to India; and the mainspring of the Raj is just power.

Thus the Teacher begins to be aware of power and its place in our earthly existence, as he never has before. Power, he realizes, is what his father and his friends were assiduously seeking in order to bring to pass their Socialist millennium. Likewise, the British Empire on which the sun never set, with India as the brightest jewel in Queen Victoria's crown, has been got together by power and is sustained by power; power is what Lenin sought and obtained to create his Dictatorship of the Proletariat, first in Russia and ultimately, as he envisaged, in the whole world. In all these enterprises, power is the essential ingredient. By contrast, Jesus proclaims His Kingdom as the antithesis of power; as a kingdom of love. Pilate and Herod and the Sanhedrin all operated in terms of power; so, on an enormously greater scale, did Caesar; but Jesus Himself disdained power, scorned it, found wisdom in babes and sucklings, and picked His disciples among fishermen. None the less, it is He, not the others, who is remembered, whose title has given two thousand years of history its name – Christendom; whose birth, ministry, death and resurrection have provided the greatest artists, writers, composers, architects, with their themes and their inspiration. Without power, He was almighty; with power the others, like fireflies, shone awhile and then disappeared.

The Teacher finds the Union Christian College a good place for meditating on such matters. Though its buildings are unfinished, they are perfectly adequate; its site is quite isolated – a bare hillside sloping down to the Perriar River where the Teacher goes for a swim each morning by way of a bath. The Raj seems very far away; its nearest representative is the British Resident whose house is in Cochin Bay, and in Cochin itself there is an ancient synagogue and a miscellaneous collection of traders from abroad.

Not in specific thinking, but in the back of his mind, deep down in his soul, the choice presents itself – power or love? quality of life or sanctity of life? comrades or brothers? Actually, the choice is made, without qualification or reservation: for love, for the sanctity of life, for brotherliness in God's human family rather than comradeship in some human cause. Made, and then buried under a great compost heap of old thoughts, stale witticisms, spent appetites and other such rubbish. Yet still the choice stands, never to be reconsidered. Such choices are the absolutes in human life; everything else may be forsaken, but they remain, impregnable for ever.

Jesus in such a contingency makes for the desert, and there subjects Himself to Satan's temptations, specially devised for so special a client. The three offered for this occasion all involve using miracles to generate power – by turning stones into bread, thereby becoming a benefactor; by jumping from the top of the Temple without hurt, thereby becoming a celebrity; by taking over all the kingdoms of the world, which, Satan claims, are in his gift, thereby becoming a worldwide dictator. Jesus turns all these offers down because they are to do with power. Thus, in His own ministry of love, fulfilling the destiny prepared for Him – to die on a cross to shouts of ribaldry and abuse in order that a great new wave of creativity should come into the world, along with a great new burgeoning of love.

> The strongest poison ever known
> Came from Caesar's laurel crown.
>
> BLAKE

I, the Captain of a Legion of Rome, serving in the desert of Libya, have learnt and pondered this truth: "There are in life but two things to be sought, Love and Power, and no one has both."

Inscription in the Libyan desert

You are the ministers of a King who cannot abdicate because He is not enthroned by the votes of men. Men did not place the crown on His head, men will not take it off. Everything falls after a time – thrones collapse, royal crowns roll in the mud. Alone the Kingdom of Christ remains standing . . . because it is guaranteed by the word of God.

Statement by the Bishop of Barcelona (Rurita) on the occasion of the foundation of the Spanish Republic, April 1931.

In 1936, during the Spanish Civil War, the Bishop was murdered.

As though to illustrate the Teacher's thoughts on the Raj and power, Gandhi pays a visit to the College. The Teacher goes to Alwaye railway station to watch his arrival. A huge crowd has gathered there to welcome him, and take the dust off his feet, mostly poor people, many of whom have trudged many miles along dusty roads to be present for the occasion. There is also a group of Untouchables, isolated from the others whom they would pollute if they were nearer together. Then the little man arrives, in a third-class carriage, wearing his loincloth, and looking like a particularly amiable gargoyle, but in the estimation of those who have turned out to welcome him, a Mahatma, a dayspring from on high that is visiting them.

At the College he speaks to the students of non-violence, of eschewing hatred, of spinning their own thread and weaving their own cloth rather than building factories and using mechanical looms. His thoughts and expectations are derived, not from revolutionary literature, but from the *Bhagavad-Gita*, the New Testament and Tolstoy's *Confessions*; his gurus are not Karl Marx or Subhas Chandra Bose, but more in the style of a Tolstoy, a Mrs Besant and the Rev. C. F. Andrews. When at last, thanks largely to his efforts, the Indian Raj takes over from the British one, to his disillusionment and disgust there is an orgy of violence and hatred. It is one more example of putting down the mighty from their seats and exalting the humble and meek, who in their turn become mighty and fit to be put down. Brown Sahibs take over from the white ones.

These are the lessons that the Teacher will have to learn in due course; for the time being he sees India's Independence and the end of the Raj as a blessed deliverance, and himself as a minor Garibaldi fanning the flames of discontent and rebellion. The most desolating part of his life at Alwaye is the classroom teaching. His subject is Eng. Lit., which he stands and expounds with a blackboard and chalk. The students have only the vaguest notion of what he is talking about, and so content themselves with memorizing his words with a view to regurgitating them when the examination comes along. Occasionally, he overhears them saying his words over and over as though they are endlessly muttering some mindless mantra. He comforts himself by supposing that this is a state of affairs peculiar to India, where, thanks to the Raj, English rather than any of the Indian vernaculars was decreed to be the language of instruction. Later, he comes to realize that the Indian situation is only an extreme version of a worldwide pattern – the pursuit of knowledge without reference to truth which alone gives knowledge its validity.

Although people seem to be unaware of it today, the development of the faculty of attention forms the real object, and almost the sole interest of studies. Quite apart from explicit religious belief, every time a human being succeeds in making an effort of attention with the sole idea of increasing his grasp of truth, he acquires a greater aptitude for grasping it even if his efforts produce no visible fruit. The other true purpose of

school studies – education – is to inculcate humility –
not just a virtue, but the condition of virtue. From this
point of view, it is perhaps even more useful to contemplate our stupidity than our sin. Studies are nearer to
God because of the attention which is their soul.

SIMONE WEIL

It is in India that the Teacher becomes sharply aware of
there being two levels of consciousness which, in his mind
and his scribbling, he specifies variously as Life and the
Legend, Imagination and Will, Reality and Fantasy, Heaven
and Hell. Having made this distinction, it seems as though
all creation mounts parables to demonstrate it to him.
Thus, for instance, when in a classroom, standing in front
of a blackboard, he is uttering banalities masquerading as
learning, he hears from a nearby paddy field the sound of
men and women singing as they work; bending over the
earth, watering, planting. So poignant are their songs – as
it might be the *Credo* in a sung Mass – that the Eng. Lit.
words die on the Teacher's lips. Again, on his evening
walks when, instead of a lingering twilight, darkness comes
down suddenly, as the curtain falls on a play that is over.
Then the lights come out, one after the other, in houses, or
where people are walking with home-made torches in their
hands, like glow-worms. The whole effect as though nature
had its own liturgy – in the paddy fields, the *Credo*; each
nightfall, a Tenebrae service.

At dawn when a still ghostly world is beginning to awake,
the Teacher goes for his morning swim; in the evening,
diving into moonlit water – like diving into light itself. And
in between, the dusty, noisy day. How to find the element
of continuity, Blake's Golden String?

How to fit together the pieces of this cosmic jigsaw
puzzle? The passing moments of a life in the setting of
Eternity; the tiny planet Earth in the setting of the Universe;

a loving God who has counted the hairs of all our heads, who cannot see a sparrow fall to the ground without concern, and the wild, ferocious story of mankind – civilizations that come and go, leaving their debris behind them for archaeologists to dig and diagnose; wars that are won and lost, philosophers who are credible and then scorned; today's beliefs, tomorrow's folly; today's hero, tomorrow's villain or idiot; Towers of Babel everlastingly being built and never finished. Thus the Teacher ruminates in the long vacation, wandering about the Nilgiri Hills, his only companion a mule loaded with his tent, his luggage and books; climbing up to summits only to see higher ones to be climbed, catching occasional glimpses of the sweltering, teeming plains below, as it might be the Kingdoms of the World as Satan spread them out before Jesus to tempt Him – in this case, the Raj, seemingly in full swing, but actually in its last decrepitude, and soon to disappear.

Perfection is nothing else than the faithful co-operation of the soul with the work of God, and begins, grows and is consummated in our souls secretly, without our being aware of it.

*

The best of all for the soul is what God wills at this particular moment, and all else must be regarded by the soul with perfect indifference as being nothing at all.

*

All that we see is lies and vanity; the truth of things is in God. What a difference between the ideas of God and our illusions!

*

All that happens in the world exists for no other purpose than the good of souls perfectly submissive to the will of God.

*

Apart from the order of God there can be no order anywhere.

*

Finding in everything only deception and nothingness, the soul is constrained to have recourse to God Himself and be content with Him.

JEAN-PIERRE DE CAUSSADE

Actually, the Teacher knows the answer, but refuses to know it, and has to keep on stifling an inner voice telling him that the answer is, in a word, the Word – God's Almighty Word, "while all things were in quiet silence, and that night was in the midst of her swift course, leaped down from Heaven out of Thy royal throne". The Word with which everything began, that came to dwell among us, full of grace and truth. The Word that is written into all truth, spoken in all wisdom, enacted in all authentic living; that is sounded in a baby's first cry, and echoes in the last rattle of death; that is embodied in the Fearful Symmetry we dare not recognize and in the sublime paradoxes we dare not utter – that children understand what sages have forgotten; that we must hate our life in this world to deserve a place in another; that the meek, not the arrogant, inherit the earth, and the foolish, not the wise, understand its caprices.

The Teacher with nothing to teach goes on his way, his mule loaded with the books he will never read, patiently following.

*   *   *

Back in England after leaving India, the Teacher gets a job as a supply-teacher in Birmingham, where he lives in a clergy house with his friend Alec Vidler. So, as in his student days, he finds himself attending services, saying liturgical prayers, and generally living in a clerical atmosphere. Then he and Kitty Dobbs get married in a registry office, deliberately making their marriage just a transaction, as it might be signing a partnership agreement, terminable by either party. (I write these words some sixty years later, with infinite thankfulness to God that in His mercy He should have allowed so fragile a plant in such barren soil to grow into so sturdy, deep-rooted and productive a tree as my marriage to Kitty, the children we begat, and the life we have shared together.)

The Teacher in the first months of married life is merely happy; happiness that comes upon us, he discovers, is as different from happiness sought or bought as is synthetic perfume from the fragrance of spring flowers. Of all the different purposes set before mankind, the most disastrous is surely "the Pursuit of Happiness", slipped into the American Declaration of Independence, along with "Life and Liberty" as an inalienable right, almost accidentally, at the last moment. "Happiness", he scribbles down, "is like a young deer, fleet and beautiful. Hunt him, and he becomes a poor frantic quarry; after the kill, a piece of stinking flesh."

True happiness, he concludes, lies in forgetfulness, not indulgence, of the self; in escape from carnal appetites, not in their satisfaction. We live in a dark, self-enclosed prison which is all we see or know if our glance is fixed downwards. To lift it upwards, becoming aware of the wide luminous universe outside – this alone is happiness. At the highest level such happiness is the ecstasy which mystics have tried to describe. At more humdrum levels, it is human love; the delights and beauties of our dear earth, its colours and shapes and sounds; the enchantment of understanding and of laughing, and all other exercises of such faculties as we possess; the marvel of the meaning of everything, fitfully glimpsed, inadequately expounded, but ever present. Such is true happiness – not compressible into a pill, nor translatable into a sensation; lost to whomever would grasp it to himself alone, not to be gorged out of a trough, or torn out of another's body, or paid into a bank, or driven along a motorway, or fired in gun salutes, or discovered in the stratosphere. Existing, intangible, in every true response to life, and absent in every false one. Propounded through the centuries in every noteworthy word and thought and deed. Expressed in art and literature, in sonorous organ recitals as in tiny melodies; in everything that is harmonious, and in the unending dedication and heroism of imperfect men reaching after perfection.

Caught up in the restlessness of the age, after some months of married life the Teacher and his wife find themselves on the banks of the Nile in Upper Egypt; then in Cairo where the Teacher is a lecturer in Eng. Lit. at the Egyptian University. His duties are not arduous, and he has plenty of time and opportunity to survey the political scene. So doing, he equates the Egyptian Nationalist movement (the Wafd) with the Indian one (Swaraj); the Egyptian leader, Nahas Pasha, with India's Mahatma Gandhi; the Egyptian effendis with the Indian babus; the Egyptian fellahin with the Indian ryots. In both countries he detects a passionate underswell in favour of universal suffrage, democracy based on One Man, One Vote. With this expertise at his fingers' ends, the Teacher sets about describing the struggle that is going on between the Pashas and Beys dozing over their hubble-bubble pipes and the toiling masses, while the ring is held by the British High Commissioner and troops, whose officers, however, show a marked preference for the Pashas and Beys. Then, on an impulse, the Teacher posts his analysis off to the *Manchester Guardian*. To his great satisfaction, it is accepted for publication, and more on the same lines is asked for and gladly provided.

In Cairo, too, a baby is born to the Teacher and his wife – a son. Looking at this tiny creature, newly come into the world, at the breast of his exhausted but triumphant mother, a sense of the glory of life sweeps through the Teacher as never before.

> My mother groaned, my father wept,
> Into the dangerous world I leapt;
> Helpless, naked, piping loud;
> Like a fiend hid in a cloud.
>
> Struggling in my father's hands,
> Striving against my swaddling bands,
> Bound and weary I thought best
> To sulk upon my mother's breast.
>
> BLAKE

This scene of a birth, enacted innumerable times in every corner of the earth, he reflects, is, after all, still the basic one – the passing on from body to body, from soul to soul, the very essence of life, as it might be a torch in some celestial Olympiad. Already he is aware of the counter-movement – the separation of the procreative impulse from procreation, the down-grading of motherhood and the up-grading of spinsterhood, and the acceptance of sterile perversions as the equivalent of fruitful lust; finally, the grisly holocaust of millions of aborted babies, ironically in the name of quality of life. The Teacher will undergo many chances of opinion, many switches of allegiance, much ethical unrest, but in one particular he will never deviate – in upholding the sanctity and the glory of life itself.

Lord, Thou that wilt not be seen but by those that be clean of heart; I have done that in me is, read and deeply thought and ensearched what it is, and on what manner I might best come to this cleanness that I might know Thee someday. Lord, I have sought and thought with all my poor head! And, Lord, in my meditation the fire of desire kindled for to know Thee, not only in the bitter dark without, but in feeling and tasting in my soul. And this worthiness I ask not for me, for I am wretched and sinful and most unworthy of all other. But, Lord, as a whelp eateth of the crumbs that fall from the board of his lord, give me of the heritage that is for to come, a drop of that heavenly joy to comfort my thirsty soul that bursteth in love-longing to Thee.

Scala Claustralium

7

The Journalist

The Liberal Mind

The Teacher continuing with his Egyptian coverage for the *Manchester Guardian*, becomes established as the paper's Cairo correspondent, and then is invited to join its editorial staff. He eagerly accepts the invitation, and the family move to Manchester. Moving from one job to another, drifting from one place to another, is for the Teacher a kind of sleep-walking of no particular significance or importance. Whatever element of continuity there may be in his life relates to quite other considerations – forgetfulness of undertakings given in his spasmodic prayers, the betrayal of visions vouch-safed him, turning aside from the inexhaustible love God offers in favour of coarse worldly satisfactions like being praised, receiving money, licking the earth.

Changing from teaching to journalism, he discovers, is not as drastic as might be supposed. Both professions are exercises in fantasy; the instruction that teachers pass on to their classes is as dubious as the news and comment that journalists pass on to their readers. Such difference as there is lies in the time factor; within reason, the Teacher can devote as much time as he likes to expounding his subject, whereas the Journalist is exclusively concerned with the immediate present. The Teacher, that is to say, is liable to be a long-drawn out bore; the Journalist, an instant one. Otherwise, they are in the same business – as St Augustine puts it, "Vendors of words".

> How miserable was I then, and how didst Thou deal with me, to make me feel my misery of that day, when I was preparing to recite a panegyric of the Emperor, wherein I was to utter many a lie, and lying, was to be applauded by those who knew I lied.
>
> St Augustine

The *Guardian*, as the Journalist discovers, is one of the last remaining Liberal strongholds, and its editor-owner, C. P. Scott, with his white vibrant beard, rubicund face, bright eyes and general impression of giving out energy, is a survivor from the days of Gladstonian glory and Lloyd-Georgian chicanery. In this setting, the Journalist is expected to turn out nightly some little editorial homily, the moral of which is that if only people at odds with one another will sit down together and talk things over, whether at some special get-together, or availing themselves of the good offices of the League of Nations (as it then was) or some kindred organization, all will be well. Thus he becomes familiar with the Liberal Mind and its working, as well as with its exponents, who come into the category, in editorialese, of "moderate men of all shades of opinion", and range between the great ones like President Woodrow Wilson, top-hatted, lantern-jawed, an ardent champion of the League of Nations, and the army of the well-intentioned – humanists, Quakers, Positivists, miscellaneous ideologues of every stripe, all resolved to abolish wars, armaments and secret diplomacy, and remove every impediment to the full realization of freedom and equality for all.

The Great Liberal Death Wish

The process of death wishing, in the guise of liberalism, has been eroding the civilization of the West for a century and more, and now would seem to be about to reach its apogee. The Liberal mind, effective everywhere, whether in power or in opposition, has provided the perfect instrument. Systematically, stage by stage, dismantling our Western way of life, depreciating and deprecating all its values so that the whole social structure is now tumbling down, dethroning its God, undermining all its certainties. And all this, wonderfully enough, in the name of the health, wealth and happiness of all mankind. Previous civilizations have been overthrown from without by the incursion of barbarian hordes; ours has dreamed up its own dissolution in the minds of its own intellectual élite. Not Bolshevism, which Stalin liquidated along with all the old Bolsheviks; not Nazism, which perished with Hitler in his Berlin bunker; not Fascism, which was left hanging upside down from a lamp-post along with Mussolini and his mistress – none of these, history will record, was responsible for bringing down the darkness on our civilization, but Liberalism. A solvent rather than a precipitate, a sedative rather than a stimulant, a slough rather than a precipice; blurring the edges of truth, the definition of virtue, the shape of beauty; a cracked bell, a mist, a death wish . . .

It was, of course, Darwin's theory of Natural Selection which first popularized the notion that Man and his environment are involved in an endless and automatic process of improvement. Who can measure the consequences of this naïve assumption? What secret subversive organization, endowed with unlimited funds and resources, could hope to achieve a thousandth part of what it achieved in the way of discrediting the then prevailing moral values and assumptions, putting in their place nothing more than vague, sentimental hopes of collective human betterment, and the Liberal Mind to entertain them? It is interesting to reflect that now, in the light of all that has happened, the early obscurantist opponents of Darwinian evolution seem vastly more sagacious and far-seeing than its early excited champions. There must be quite a number today who would rather go down to history even as puffing, portentous Bishop Wilberforce than, say, a Herbert Spencer, or a poor, squeaky H. G. Wells, ardent evolutionist and disciple of Huxley, with his vision of an earthly paradise achieved through science and technology; those twin monsters which have laid waste a whole world, polluting its seas and rivers and lakes with poisons, infecting its very earth and all its creatures, reaching into Man's mind and inner consciousness to control and condition him, at the same time entrusting to irresponsible, irresolute human hands the instruments of universal destruction. It must be added that, confronted with this prospect when, at the very end of his life, the first nuclear explosion was announced, Wells turned his face to the wall, letting off in *Mind at the end of its Tether* one last, despairing, whimpering cry which unsaid everything he had ever thought or hoped. Belatedly, he understood that what he had followed as a life-force was, in point of fact, a death wish, into which he was glad to sink the little that remained of his own life in the confident expectation of total and final obliteration.

The enthronement of the gospel of progress necessarily required the final discrediting of the Gospel of Christ, and the destruction of the whole edifice of ethics, law, culture, human relationships and human behaviour constructed upon it. What we continue to call Western Civilization, after all, began with Christian revelation, not the theory of evolution, and, we may be sure, will perish with it, too – if it has not already. Jesus of Nazareth was its founding father, not Charles Darwin; it was Paul of Tarsus who first carried its message to Europe, not Karl Marx, or even Lenin. Jesus, by dying on the Cross, abolished death wishing; dying became thenceforth life's glory and fulfilment. So, when Jesus called on His followers to die in order to live, He created a tidal wave of joy and hope on which they have ridden for two thousand years. The gospel of progress represents the exact antithesis. It plays the Crucifixion backwards, as it were; in the beginning was the flesh, and the flesh became Word. In the light of this Logos in reverse, the quest for hope is the ultimate hopelessness; the pursuit of happiness, the certitude of despair; the lust for life, the embrace of death . . .

It is, indeed, among Christians themselves that the final decisive assault on Christianity has been mounted. All they had to show was that when Jesus said that His kingdom was not of this world, He meant that it was. Then, moving on from there, to stand the other basic Christian propositions similarly on their heads. As, that to be carnally minded is life; that it is essential to lay up treasure on earth in the shape of a constantly expanding Gross National Product; that the flesh lusts with the spirit and the spirit with the flesh, so that we can do whatever we have a mind to; that he that loveth his life in this world shall keep it unto life eternal. And so on . . .

In the moral vacuum left by thus emptying Christianity of its spiritual or transcendental content, the great Liberal Death Wish has been able to flourish and luxuriate; the more so because it can plausibly masquerade as aiming at its opposite – life enhancement. Furthermore, the announcement on the best theological authority that God has died removes any possibility of intervention from that quarter. So the astronauts soar into the vast eternities of space, on earth the garbage piles higher; as the groves of academe extend their domain, their alumni's arms reach lower; as the phallic cult spreads, so does impotence. In great wealth, great poverty; in health, sickness; in numbers, deception. Gorging, left hungry; sedated, left restless; telling all, hiding all; in flesh united, forever separate. So we press on through the valley of abundance that leads to the wasteland of satiety, passing through the gardens of fantasy; seeking happiness ever more ardently, and finding despair ever more surely.

Each evening in their little perches along the editorial corridor, the Journalist and the other leader-writers prepare their homilies – shorts, two-pars and longs. The structure is invariable; first, the subject has to be stated – say, rioting in Calcutta (the Journalist rates as an expert on Indian matters). Then a comment – it is understandable, but unfortunate, that the Indian nationalists, rightly struggling to be free, should resort to violence. Finally, a solution – Let the Viceroy and Mahatma Gandhi get together and work out a basis for a peaceful transfer of power from the Raj to the Indian people, along with the institution of Parliamentary Government based on one man, one vote, and majority rule. Then the association between India and Britain, forcibly imposed in the first place, will continue by mutual consent, to the advantage of both countries. The Journalist reads over what he has written, and is well content. So is the Editor, who is pleased to note that the latest addition to his staff can turn in the right stuff. Walking home at night through deserted Manchester streets when the paper has been put to bed, the sentences lose their lustre and echo emptily in the Journalist's mind.

It is summer-time, and already faint traces of light are appearing in the sky. Surely, he reflects, there must be more in life than pious expectations that in Delhi, as in Westminster, Mr Speaker wearing a wig will preside over Honourable and Right Honourable Members as they shout at one another in their various vernaculars. Once again he is overwhelmed by a sense of there being some other dimension of living – call it God! – some other version of Time – call it Eternity! – some other way than dark, empty streets leading from nowhere to nowhere – call it the Way of the Lord whose paths must be made straight. In the beginning was the Word – a catch phrase that seems to say something momentous. But what Word? Whose Word? If there was a beginning, to what end? Such questions gather round the Journalist and suffocate him. How to answer them? Where is God? Without finding Him, how to know Him? The clocks tick on but never register Eternity. Without a signpost, how to find the way? Among all the babble of words, written, spoken, whispered, orated, chanted, how to pick out *the* Word?

The answer is lurking about in the Journalist's mind, half-formed; at once too wonderful and too preposterous to be believed – that God could become a Man in a particular place and at a particular time; that this having happened, God who was a Man, or, amounting to the same thing, a Man who was God, could be nailed to a cross and left to die, only to rise from the dead, and, after spending a few days with His disciples, then a brief sojourn in hell, disappear into heaven, there to watch over mankind for evermore. Who in his right mind could believe such a story? Well, to begin with, all those who have believed it. That is to say, the greatest artists, mystics, sculptors, saints, builders – for instance, builders of the great medieval cathedrals –

over the Christian centuries, not to mention the Christians of all sorts and conditions whose lives, generation after generation, have been irradiated, given a meaning and a direction, through this great drama of the birth, ministry, death and resurrection of Jesus of Nazareth. In any case, the Journalist gleefully asks himself, who would not rather be wrong with St Francis of Assisi, St Augustine of Hippo, all the saints and mystics for two thousand years, not to mention Dante, Michelangelo, Shakespeare, Milton, Pascal, than right with Bernard Shaw, H. G. Wells, Karl Marx, Nietzsche, the Huxleys, Bertrand Russell and such like? By this time the Journalist has reached his front door, and abruptly breaks off his reverie. The next morning he picks up the day's *Guardian*, duly delivered, and reads over his leader – now captioned: INDIA – THE NEXT STEP? – several times with the utmost satisfaction.

Waiting on God

In the stress of life, collectively in the chaos of politics, individually in the clamorous demands of the ego and the flesh, it is always open to us to wait on God. All we have to do is, as it were, to make a little clearing in the wild jungle of our human will, and then keep our rendezvous with our Creator. He is sure to come; His presence falls like a comforting shadow, and then we are at peace. Our tiny exercise in Time is lost in the immensity of Eternity; as Blake puts it: "All the world in a grain of sand, infinity in the palm of your hand."

This experience is open to anyone at any time – fighting one's way on to a crowded commuter train, forcing tired eyes to grapple with turgid words, sleepless in an interminable night; and then, suddenly and incalculably, peace; the acceptance of earthly circumstances; all the turbulence, doubt, conflicting devices and desires; crystallizing in one single prayer: "Thy will be done."

*

"Vanity Fair is closing down."

*

"A treasure-trove of artificial pearls."

*

God signifies an alternative impulse – to sacrifice rather than grab, to love rather than lust, to give rather than take, to pursue truth rather than promote lies, to humble oneself rather than inflate the ego. In all creation the hand of God is seen; in every human heart, in a blade of grass as in great trees and mountains and rivers; in the first stirring of life in a foetus and in the last musings and mutterings of a tired mind.

* * *

Already the Journalist is struck by the contrast between what is actually happening in the world and the presentation of it in the *Guardian* and the Media generally. This is a theme that will occupy his mind for many years to come, with the development of each new means of presentation – radio, television in all its developments – widening the gap between events themselves and their projected images. For instance, the proceedings of Parliament, which from time to time the Journalist has occasion to observe and follow from the Press Gallery. There, beneath him, on the floor of the House of Commons, was being fulfilled the dream of his father and his friends as they had entertained and discussed it in his childhood years. A Labour Government in power, a Labour Prime Minister in Downing Street, and a Labour Chancellor of the Exchequer next door, and a legislative programme in hand for bringing to pass a kingdom of heaven on earth as envisaged – no more exploitation of man by man, no more injustice, poverty, war; only brotherliness and peace. If the mighty had not yet been actually put down from their seats, they soon would be; if the humble and meek had not yet been exalted, they were well on the way, as was exemplified by the Prime Minister, Ramsay MacDonald, whose rolling "R"'s, woebegone moustache and floating hair embodied the popular view of an inspired revolutionary. Behind him sit his supporters, among them the Journalist's father, now an MP, and opposite the Prime Minister, his opponents – Mr Baldwin, two Chamberlains, one monocled and the other not, and Winston Churchill.

Returning to the Press Gallery some weeks later, the parliamentary situation is drastically changed. MacDonald is still Prime Minister, but in a so-called National Government his associates now are the Tory and Liberal leaders who were formerly the Opposition, whereas his late colleagues glower at him from the Opposition benches. The new Government's policy is to sustain our currency – God save our gracious pound! Long live our noble pound! – and to ensure that God who has made us mighty will make us mightier yet. The Journalist finds himself infected with the prevailing excitement generated by such a political about-face; taps furiously at his typewriter, rushes to the telephone, engages in whispered conversations with his fellow journalists, as well as with Hon. Members, and even, when possible, Rt Hon. ones.

Then, in bed and sleepless, he goes over it all again; hears the Prime Minister announcing with gusto: "And when we find quackeries we shall expose quackeries!" – he the greatest quack ever; watches in the division lobbies strange new partners, and notes how his father's face is aghast at what has happened. All this, he decides, is fatuity recollected in tranquillity, creating a condition of schizophrenia. On the one hand, a Theatre of the Absurd, a Chaplinesque performance, a harlequinade, as though the figures of the great ones in Madame Tussaud's Exhibition – Prime Ministers and Presidents, a solid phalanx of Royalty, eminent murderers, Popes and celebrated mummers and clowns – came to life and did their own little acts. On the other hand, what?

The Theatre of Fearful Symmetry

Tiger! Tiger! burning bright
In the forest of the night,
What immortal hand or eye
Could frame thy fearful symmetry?

BLAKE

It is in considering this question that the Journalist discovers that what he had taken to be a Theatre of the Absurd proves on closer examination to contain within itself a Theatre of Fearful Symmetry. The fantasy of the world as presented in the Theatre of the Absurd remains; it also says something, thereby transforming itself into a Theatre of Fearful Symmetry, and revealing the meaning that lies embedded in meaninglessness, the order underlying confusion, the indestructible love at the heart of the holocaust of hate, the still, small voice of truth that makes itself heard above thunderous falsity.

So, the Journalist gets into the habit of straining his ears to catch what the Theatre of Fearful Symmetry has to say, and of straining his eyes, as he looks through, not with, them, to see what it has to show. Far from eroding the comedy, this enhances it, to the point that laughter engulfs everything; coming in from all directions – equally in steeples climbing into the sky as in gargoyles grinning and jeering down at the earth. Reaching upwards, the Journalist is a steeple, though a paltry and rickety one; peering downwards, he is a gargoyle, straining to break through the Ego barrier into the wide glorious reaches of God's laughter, where such as Cervantes's Knight of the Woeful Countenance, Shakespeare's Sir John Falstaff, Gogol's Chichikov, P. G. Wodehouses's Jeeves and Bertie Wooster, have their being.

The Steeple and the Gargoyle

Newcomers to the Christian faith, the Journalist finds, are considered, by the nature of the case, to have lost their sense of humour: How funny he used to be! and now, alas, how solemn! how portentous! What an unconscionable bore he has become! This assumption that a sense of humour and a Christian faith are incompatible is totally mistaken. In point of fact the writers of the great classics of humour – like Rabelais, Cervantes, Swift, Gogol – have all been deeply religious. Even comedians, like Bob Hope, tend to be believers rather than sceptics or cynics. This applies even to a poor, crazed Lenny Bruce. It is the millionaires and pornographers and megalomaniacs, and doctrinaire politicians and sociologists and abortionists, people of that stamp, who wrap themselves in solemnity, and wince at the sound of laughter. "That idiot laughter, a passion hateful to our purpose", Shakespeare's King John says, speaking on behalf of all tyrants everywhere and at all times, anointed and ideological.

The true function of humour is to express in terms of the grotesque the immense disparity between human aspiration and human performance. Mysticism expresses the same disparity in terms of the sublime. Hence the close connection between clowns and mystics; hence, too, the juxtaposition on the great medieval cathedrals of steeples reaching up into the Cloud of Unknowing, and gargoyles grinning malevolently down at our dear earth and all its foolishness. Laughter and mystical ecstasy, that is to say, both derive from an awareness, in the one case hilarious, in the other ecstatic, of how wide is the chasm between Time and Eternity, between us and our Creator.

Let us then, while, as we should, revering the steeples, remember the gargoyles, also, in their way, purveyors of God's Word, and be thankful that, when the Gates of Heaven swing open, as they do from time to time, mixed with the celestial music there is the unmistakable sound of celestial laughter.

Shakespeare gives some of his best lines to his fools — for instance, to the Fool in *King Lear* and to Caliban in *The Tempest*. So does God, as the Apostle Paul indicates when he points out that God has made foolish the wisdom of this world, and that the foolishness of God is wiser than men.

How wonderful it is, this marrying of the ribaldry of gargoyles with the sublimity of steeples, this seeing of a saint in every clown and a clown in every saint, and the Fall of Man as being, at once, the measure and fatality of all our afflictions and the old banana-skin joke on a cosmic scale. Who but a God who had deigned to become incarnate could arrange things so? Encompassing in His love the suffering and the absurdity of His creation; including in one scenario steeples reaching heavenwards and gargoyles grinning and grimacing earthwards, in one mercy the affliction which is our lot and the capacity to laugh with Rabelais in the person of Panurge at the antics of carnal men, with Cervantes in the person of Don Quixote at the antics of crusading men, with Shakespeare in the person of Sir John Falstaff at the antics of mortal men. Laughter, indeed, is God's therapy; He planted the steeples and the gargoyles, gave us clowns as well as saints, in order that we might understand that at the heart of our mortal existence there lies a mystery, at once unutterably beautiful and hilariously funny.

Once more, it is borne in upon the Journalist that throughout every moment of existence God is trying to say something to us if only we will listen; that in every happening, large and small, from the bite of a flea to a nuclear explosion, from a muttered word while sleeping to Beethoven's symphonies, the Creator speaks to His creation. This realization does not come about suddenly; gradually, insensibly, the Journalist becomes aware that all he has to do is to listen, which means having ears to hear, being tuned into the requisite wavelength. Like a radio operator in the *Maquis*, he picks up a variety of sounds on his receiving set – music, news, orations, in all sorts of languages and voices. Then his attentive ear catches the agreed signal; he is all alert; the sounds signify something at last. Even then, as St Augustine points out, there is the difficulty that we can only communicate in words which have a beginning and an end, and so cannot convey what never began and cannot end – Eternity in terms of time, immortality in terms of mortality.

Returning to the sound of our own tongue

One day Augustine and his mother, Monica,
    stood alone, by a window, which looked inwards to
    the garden within the house where they were staying.
    "There we talked together, she and I alone, in deep
    joy . . . And while we were thus talking of His wisdom
    and panting for it, with all the effort of our heart we
    did for one instant attain to touch it; then, sighing,
    and leaving the first fruits of our spirits bound to it,
    *we returned to the sound of our own tongue, in which
    words must have a beginning and an end* . . . Thus we

spoke: If to any man the tumult of the flesh grew silent, silent the images of earth and sea and air; and if the heavens grew silent, and the very soul grew silent to herself, and, by not thinking of self, mounted beyond self; if all dreams and images grew silent, and every tongue and every symbol – everything that passes away . . . and in their silence He alone spoke to us, not by them, but by Himself; so that we should hear His word, not by any tongue of the flesh, not in the voices of an angel, not in the sound of thunder, nor in the darkness of a parable – but that we should hear Himself . . . should hear Himself and not them. . . . 'Son,' Monica says, 'what do I here any longer, and to what end am I here, I know not, now that my hopes in this world are accomplished. One thing there was for which I desired to linger for a while in this life, that I might see thee a Catholic Christian before I died. My God hath done this for me most abundantly, that I should see thee withal, despising earthly happiness, become His servant: *What do I here?*'"

The Journalist finds himself addressing this same question to himself with ever greater insistence – What do I here?

A mood of melancholy settles upon the Journalist. In Lancashire unemployment mounts steadily; Ramsay Mac-Donald's so-called National Government goes to the country, and is returned with an overwhelming majority, leaving the Labour Opposition with only a handful of MPs. Among the large number of Labour Members defeated at the hustings is the Journalist's father. In these circumstances, going on expressing in the *Guardian*'s leader columns vague hopes that the Liberal Mind may yet save the situation, grows ever more irksome. The moderate men of all shades of opinion to whom such editorials are addressed, are hard to come by, whereas immoderate men of no shades of opinion markedly proliferate. At the same time, the ostensible Man of Destiny, the Prime Minister, despite an unprecedented electoral victory, increasingly gives an impression of being witless and incoherent; put a butterfly net in his hands and he is perfectly cast as a crazed botany professor; as an orator, he is Dryden's Doeg to the life:

> Free from all meaning, whether good or bad,
> And in one word, heroically mad.

In these circumstances, the Journalist is more than ever prone to secret praying; whether sudden ejaculations while walking along a road – "Help me! Guide me! Use me!", or more considered efforts, some of which he subsequently scribbles down.

Prayer

Prayer, the Church's banquet, Angels' Age,
    God's breath in man returning to his birth,
    The soul in paraphrase, heart in pilgrimage
The Christian plummet, sounding heaven and earth,
Engine against the Almighty, sinner's tower,
    Reversed thunder, Christ-side-piercing spear,
    The six-days world transposing in an hour,
A kind of tune, which all things hear and fear;
Softness, and peace, and joy, and love, and bliss,
    Exalted manna, gladness of the best,
    Heaven in ordinary, man well drest,
The milky way, the bird of paradise,
    Church bells beyond the stars heard, the soul's
      blood,
    The land of spices, something understood.

GEORGE HERBERT

God, humble my pride, extinguish the last stirrings of my Ego, obliterate whatever remains of worldly ambition and carnality, and help me to serve only Thy purposes, to speak and write only Thy words, to think only Thy thoughts, to have no other prayer than "Thy will be done".

I can do nothing alone; my own will, however hard I exert it, does not suffice; my own plans, however astutely and systematically devised, all fail. So, there is nothing for it but to hand myself over to God, truly and wholly, so that He may use, or, for that matter, in His wisdom not use, whatever capacity I possess to serve Him. And, since I cannot see or converse with Him, I turn to Jesus Christ, the Mediator, for guidance and support.

Behold, O Lord, my poor heart which through your goodness has conceived many great desires but is too weak and wretched to put them into practice unless You grant Your heavenly grace. This I beg, O Merciful Father, through the Passion of Thy Son to whose honour I consecrate this and all my days.

ST FRANCIS DE SALES

I myself see Christianity today as the only living spiritual force capable of undertaking the spiritual healing of Russia.

In moments of weakness and distress it is good to tread closely in God's footsteps.

ALEXANDER SOLZHENITSYN

Religious faith is the acceptance of the mystery of our existence here on earth, science being the antithesis of this — the conviction that somehow, sometime the alleged "facts of life", how we came to be, what we are, and to what end, will all be elucidated. Hence the ludicrous theories propounded and expounded, and the wild controversies about them — as, the Big Bang against the notion of continuous creation, and, above all, Darwinian evolution, a very rickety hypothesis based on some old bones or a tooth discovered in Kenya or Nanking, and infiltrating all the different disciplines of learning, and making an ultimate nonsense of them all.

God arises because we cannot do anything alone. We are too weak and variable and helpless. Even just to take charge of our own bodies is impossible without outside help. Existence itself becomes impossible without God. To the minute degree that I have been able to lift my head out of the trough round which we humans so furiously and so avidly gather, it has been entirely due to God's help. If this had been lacking (and of course it never is) I should have lived wholly in darkness, in "licking the earth!"

*

There is no holiness, Lord, if you withdraw your hand. No wisdom is of any use if you no longer guide it. No strength can avail if you do not preserve it. No purity is safe if you do not protect it. No watchfulness on our part can affect anything unless your holy vigilance is present with us. If you abandon us, we sink and perish; but if you come to us we are raised up and we live.

THOMAS À KEMPIS

Every sort of fighting and strife, among individuals or between collectivities, is about power, sex or money — all, in themselves, quite worthless things.

The Journalist finds himself often saying over to himself the only prayer he knows by heart, the Lord's Prayer. So doing, he grasps how much is packed into this brief masterpiece of words. The dreams of his father and his friends, along with many others, of an earthly paradise, become an irrelevance, and it has to be accepted that the earthly cities which men build and men destroy can never become the City of God which they did not build and cannot destroy. They only function as a staging-post in the unfolding and coming to pass of God's purposes for His creation. Thus veritably is God's will done on earth as in heaven, and always will be. As for what we are to look for on our own behalf – and this is particularly beautiful – it is the least of earthly favours; no more than that we should be given this day our daily bread. Then there is forgiveness. Yes, we ask to be forgiven, but only to the extent that we forgive those who offend us – a brilliantly subtle arrangement. Finally, to overcome the temptations the world offers us, to shed our pride, our greed, our lust, our covetousness by our own efforts, is beyond our capacity. So, we ask not to be led into temptation, remembering how Bunyan's Pilgrim, after having coped with Doubting Castle, the Slough of Despond, and even the Valley of the Shadow of Death, still finds it necessary to shut his eyes and stop his ears as he runs through Vanity Fair.

In addition to saying his prayers, the Journalist discovers that they are indeed answered; not always in the way he might hope for or expect, but still answered. He finds it extraordinary that they should be so answered, just by waiting for a response, which, when it comes, is perfectly adjusted to the request. In the deeply troubled times he is living through he grieves that he should be expending all his energies on following what is going on – reading the newspapers, and otherwise heeding the Media, arguing and declaiming. Then a kind of passion takes possession of him, and all sorts of apprehensions gather round, so that he cannot sleep, or, waking in the night, he is troubled by the thought of work undone, commitments made and not fulfilled, an overwhelming sense of his total inadequacy. Somehow he spells out the Lord's Prayer, and asks to be taken over so that his remaining days or months or even years may be wholly taken over by our Creator, or by Jesus on behalf of our Creator. Nothing happens; he continues to be lost and hopeless, until, hours later, the answer comes in the shape of illumination, enabling him to understand perfectly that history is to mankind precisely what the experience of living is to an individual – that is to say, a drama to be lived through. We do not write the script, nor do we choose our allotted parts; what is required of us is to speak our lines, make our entrances and our exits, until the curtain falls and our role is for the time being exhausted.

So, there are not good times and bad, worthy rulers and unworthy; nor is there progress and recession. As the Apostle Paul tells us, all authority should be accepted, and all overturning of authority equally accepted as being ordained of God. Our business is to find God, the dramatist behind the drama, and, having found Him, to follow Him in the light of the revelation vouchsafed us in the birth, ministry, death and resurrection of Jesus Christ. Understanding this, the Journalist's whole being is suffused with light and joy. Now he has no care in the world; now no fellow man is other than his dear brother, no woman other than his dear sister, and he seems to hear spoken almost the last words Jesus uttered on earth: "In this world ye shall have tribulation, but be of good cheer, I have overcome the world."

Envisaging the possibility of a good government is a dangerous illusion, and, indeed, virtually ensures the installation of a bad one. When has the overthrowing of a government installed a better one in its place? Is France a better place for having had a revolution? Or America? Or Russia? In recent years more governments have been overturned than in any comparable period of history, and in the process the confusion, violence, oppression, privation, servitude, bloodshed and injustice in the world have steadily augmented. If, however, we follow the Apostle Paul's guidance, and accept authority whatever it may be (in his case, the Emperor Nero's), within its own terms of reference, we are free to concern ourselves with the two basic rules of conduct laid down in the New Testament – to love God and our neighbour. St Paul in the end, if the traditional story is to be believed, was destroyed by Nero, but this would not have altered his opinion that Nero's government, as the existing one, had to be accepted. Had he not taken this view, and followed, say, the example of Spartacus, he might have thereby rated a footnote in the history books, but he would assuredly not have founded a religion, a Church and a civilization which has lasted till the present day, and is now on the point of expiring largely because the dogma that our human condition can be ameliorated by the exercise of power has come to be almost universally accepted.

> I no longer wished for a better world because I was thinking of the whole of creation, and in the light of this clearer discernment I have come to see that, though the higher things are better than the lower, the sum of all creation is better than the higher things alone.
>
> St Augustine

The Journalist is subject to nightmares which, though they differ in detail, all have the same essential pattern – viz. that he has lost his way, does not know where he is or who he is. Blake, in his mysterious way, perfectly conveys what this amounts to – "The lost traveller's dream under the Hill". A recurrent Kafkaesque situation is of being imprisoned, why he cannot tell; he shouts for help, but no one hears him, and once, in the course, as he imagined, of escaping, he put his fist through a window, thereby opening a vein and awaking in a cascade of blood. The dark cell in which he is imprisoned is tiny, with no room to move; the darkness seems impenetrable and everlasting, with no trace of a dawn to come. He is manacled and helpless, and his cries for help just echo back to him. Then suddenly he becomes aware that, after all, there *is* a glimmer of light coming through some sort of window; that his manacles are satanic purposes – his lechery, his greed, his pride, his covetousness; that the cell in which he is imprisoned is no other than his own Ego. If only he could get to the window! If only he could shake off his manacles! If only he could extricate himself from his Ego-container! Would he not find himself in "the glorious liberty of the children of God"? The phrase runs through his head, and takes over his heart. He thinks of all the different kinds of freedom being canvassed in his time – freedom to eat, drink and be merry, libertine freedom in all its aspects – and contrasts them with this other glorious liberty available to God's children. Thereupon the lost traveller under the hill is no longer lost; he has found his way, and his dream has come true.

By this time the Journalist has wearied of his leader-writing on the *Manchester Guardian*. All through his life he is dogged by his tendency to lose interest in whatever he may have taken on in the way of work, and then to sink into a mood of melancholy and hopelessness. Of the seven deadly sins, *accidie* – defined as "a state of restlessness and inability to work or pray" – is the one to which he is most prone. Life loses its savour, and even its passing interest; the words which are his livelihood fall like dead leaves on a bleak November day. God disappears, and cries to Him for help just echo emptily back. In these circumstances, change seems the only recourse – to go somewhere else, do something else, be someone else. It is admittedly only a temporary alleviation, like getting drunk or falling in love. Thus the Journalist manages to get transferred from being on the *Guardian*'s editorial staff in Manchester to being its Moscow correspondent.

The Tsar is dead; long live Stalin!

For the Journalist his arrival in Moscow was meant to be
a moment of great exhilaration; like going for the first time
into the Sistine Chapel, or coming upon the Egyptian
pyramids or the Taj Mahal. With some difficulty he manages to work up some sort of emotional response, but it is
simulated; in reality he finds that the wonders of the world
are not, to him, all that wonderful, but a kind of etiquette
requires that they should be so regarded. Thus the Journalist
does his best, inducing himself to believe that in Russia for
the first time in human history the "people" own their
own environment, direct their own purposes, and may be
expected to behave accordingly. On his first visit to Red
Square, standing in front of the Kremlin over which the
Red Flag flies perpetually, he finds himself mentally writing
a leading article – "Whatever view may be taken of such
developments as the institution of secret political police,
known at first as the Cheka and now as the GPU, and
based precisely on the notorious Okhrana of Tsarist times,
the fact remains that the regime Lenin constructed on
the ruins of Tsarism, and that his successor, Stalin, has
taken over and strengthened, may now be said to have
established itself. For good or ill the world has to reckon
with a new factor in government – the Dictatorship of the
Proletariat."

Darkness is falling on Red Square, but the Journalist
continues walking up and down it with his mind in a state
of turmoil. Now the Red Flag, caught in a searchlight, is
like blood staining a black sky. Opposite the Kremlin there
is a large baroque building, formerly the Russian Orthodox
Cathedral of St Basil and now an anti-God museum, whose
interior is dominated by a metal ball swinging to and fro
to illustrate the force of gravity, and seen as abolishing the
notion of a God or the need for one. On display, also, there

are the fossilized remains of saints dug out of their tombs to confound the superstition that their bodies are not subject to decay. As part of the same ensemble, there is Lenin's mausoleum where the little man's embalmed corpse in an airtight glass case is on display, minus the brain, which is said to be pickled and deposited elsewhere. Is this, the Journalist wonders, another superstition in process of being built up, whose authenticity will doubtless in due course also be called in question? To see for himself, he joins the interminable queue of Soviet citizens and visitors which forms outside the mausoleum, waiting to pay their respects to the founding father of the USSR, or just to stare at him as he lies with his head on a red velvet cushion and his body lost in the khaki tunic he is wearing with its single decoration – the Order of Lenin.

Red Square becomes for the Journalist, as it were, a godless retreat to which he repairs from time to time to sort out his impressions and formulate conclusions. Much of his time is spent just walking about the streets of Moscow and looking at the faces of passers-by, trying to reconstruct their daily lives – standing in queues at shops and metro stations, putting up with overcrowded housing, suppressing irritation at shortages of pretty well everything except vodka, constantly aware of the GPU, whose omnipresence reaches out from the Lubianka to cover the whole city. Is it a romantic fancy, the Journalist asks himself, that somehow all this deprivation of one sort and another gives their faces a kind of nobility and even beauty? Is suffering in their case a special kind of blessing, so that far from beating their breasts over it they are exalted? Mysteriously, the cross full of glory seems to haunt the first city in the West to have abolished it, to the point that the Journalist almost expects the Cathedral transformed into an anti-God museum to overflow with the poignant notes of the Russian Orthodox Mass.

Thus, wandering about the streets of Moscow and rubbing shoulders with its citizens, mysteriously, the Journalist comes to see as never before that in suffering and deprivation rather than in well-being and ease the light of understanding shines forth; that in humility, not pride, the eyes see and the ears hear what the experience of living truly signifies. The Man on the Cross dying to ribald shouts and mockery is validated, and seen to have guided and inspired through the Christian centuries all that is most creative and wonderful in human life. For an instant or two the Journalist sees clearly, so that his whole being is full of ecstasy; then, like St Augustine and his mother, Monica, he returns to the sound of his own tongue in which words have a beginning and an end.

In this case, the return involves moving into the Kremlin itself where there is a meeting of the Supreme Soviet, to whose opening session foreign journalists are admitted. The hall is crowded with delegates from all over the USSR; on the platform sit the Politbureau, clustered together for comfort, both physical and ideological. There is an air of expectancy; at a given signal all rise to their feet and begin clapping as Stalin, with his queer waddling walk, makes his way to an empty seat at the centre of the stage. Even the foreign journalists look with a certain awe at his arrival on the scene, and some of them in a vague lost sort of way join in the clapping, which is being timed by GPU officers to ensure that it lasts for the regulation seven minutes. Even, however, when the signal has been given that now seven minutes are up, and the clapping can stop, it still goes on a while as no one wants to be seen as the first who stops. Only when Stalin has settled into his chair does the applause finally die down and the business of the meeting begin.

> The hand of vengeance found the bed
> To which the purple tyrant fled,

The iron hand crushed the tyrant's head
  And became a tyrant in his stead.

B<small>LAKE</small>

In five years I shall possess the entire world.

One cannot lie in the bed of kings without catching from them the madness of destruction. I too have gone mad.

Thought is the foremost enemy of a monarch.

N<small>APOLEON</small>

Stalin, as things turned out, will soon be disposing of most of his colleagues with him on the platform by handing them over to the GPU for interrogation, in the certainty that they will be induced to confess to treasonable views and activities. Then, in due course, they will be taken away and shot, leaving Stalin to reign alone; another Tsar, to take Russia back to traditional imperialism and anti-Semitism, and even in some degrees revive the Russian Orthodox Church, its liturgy and its dignitaries.

Brooding on this macabre harlequinade of power, more evident in the USSR even than in India under the British Raj, the Journalist turns his attention to another scene – Jesus in the wilderness being offered the kingdoms of the world by the Devil in person, who claims to have them in his gift, and makes no other condition for handing them over than that Jesus should abandon God and worship him, the Devil! What an opportunity for anyone with Utopian expectations to close with this offer, set up a kingdom of heaven on earth, and live happily ever after! Jesus, however, turns the offer down, on the ground that worshipping the Devil can only have devilish consequences. As an alternative to the kingdoms of the world, He proclaims a kingdom *not* of this world, where pride gives place to humility, and the quest for power becomes a quest for love – all this, not just in words, but embodied in the great drama of the Incarnation.

Following this line of thought, the Journalist comes to grasp that the climax of Jesus's earthly ministry, His Crucifixion, amounted to a *reductio ad absurdum* of what the Devil has on offer – which is power. Likewise, Pilate's ironical billing of Jesus on the Cross as "King of the Jews" misfires in the light of Jesus's true destiny as "God's Almighty Word leaping down from Heaven out of His Royal Throne". Again, the mockery of the Roman soldiers misfires when they dress Jesus up in a scarlet robe, put a crown of thorns on His head, give Him a reed to hold in His hand as a sceptre, and then kneel down before Him in obeisance, chanting: "Hail, King of the Jews!" The soldiers are not, as they suppose, just ridiculing a poor, distraught and deluded man about to be crucified, but holding up to ridicule all who exercise power, thereby making power itself derisory, so that thenceforth thorns will be woven into every crown, and under every scarlet robe there will be stricken flesh.

Thus the Theatre of Fearful Symmetry, but, the Journalist observes, the Theatre of the Absurd is also in full swing as the fine flower of the Liberal intelligentsia of the Western world see in the Soviet regime a new dawn breaking, and in Stalin the twentieth century's Man of Destiny . . .

Stalin

Stalin, seated with his Politbureau associates, sombre, full of energy, dark hair growing low on his forehead, and small dark eyes set closely together. A gloomy, lonely, barbarous figure, more Asiatic than European; on the whole, though, more impressive than Lenin's pink head in its glass case in his mausoleum. The pink head, after all, might have bobbed about quite happily in parliamentary lobbies and committee rooms; on government and opposition benches. In the long run it might have turned out to be an Honourable, or even Right Honourable pink head. Stalin is different. He has never chattered away evenings in dingy lodgings, or spent indigestive afternoons playing chess in cafés in Vienna, or loitered, a proletarian rentier or remittance man, by the Lake of Geneva. He can become, and remain, the Dictatorship of the Proletariat in person because he so hates and despises the proletariat. Product of a Tiflis theological seminary, a home-bred, class-war Napoleon.

The rest who constitute the Dictatorship of the Proletariat are shadowy enough; mediocrities capable of flattering and of effacing themselves; echoes more or less distinct; a curious company, ghostly, unreal; spending their days together in the Kremlin; reading newspapers they have written years ago, written and forgotten; seeing everywhere their own portraits and busts, and hearing everywhere applause, half-believing and half-afraid; utterly apart, not only from all the world in general, but from Russia, from Moscow; they, too, embalmed and preserved in a vacuum; dim, superannuated tyrants with memories of old victories and enthusiasms, and fear for the future; anxious tyrants whose very arrogance is thin and apprehensive; shadows filling an empty space where the Dictatorship of the Proletariat is supposed to be.

Friends of the Soviet Union

Liberal minds flocked to the USSR in an unending procession, from the great ones like Shaw and Gide and Barbusse and Julian Huxley and Harold Laski and Sidney and Beatrice Webb, down to poor little teachers, crazed clergymen and millionaires, drivelling dons, all utterly convinced that, under the aegis of the great Stalin, a new dawn is breaking in the world, so that the human race may at last be united in liberty, equality and fraternity for evermore . . . These Liberal minds are prepared to believe anything, however preposterous, to overlook anything, however villainous, to approve anything, however obscurantist and brutally authoritarian, in order to be able to preserve intact the confident expectation that one of the most thoroughgoing, ruthless and bloody tyrannies ever to exist on earth can be relied on to champion human freedom, the brotherhood of man, and all the other good Liberal causes to which they had dedicated their lives . . .

They are unquestionably one of the marvels of the age; the spectacle is unforgettable of them travelling with radiant optimism through a famished countryside, wandering in happy bands about squalid, overcrowded towns, listening with unshakeable faith to the outpourings of carefully trained Intourist guides, repeating, like school children their multiplication tables, the bogus statistics and monotonous slogans that are fed interminably to Soviet citizens. There, no doubt, some office-holder in the League of Nations Union; there a godly Quaker who once had tea with Gandhi; there an inveigher against the Blasphemy Laws; there a staunch upholder of free-speech and free-trade; there a preventer of cruelty to animals; there scarred and worthy veterans of a hundred battles for truth, peace and freedom, all, all chanting the praises of the Dictatorship of the Proletariat, and of Stalin as its most gracious and beloved figurehead. It was as though a Salvation Army contingent had turned out with bands and banners in honour of some ferocious tribal deity, or as though a vegetarian society had issued a passionate plea for cannibalism.

For man exists only if he is an image and reflection of God, he exists only if God exists. Let God be nonexistent, let man make of himself a God and no longer a man – his proper image will perish. *The only solution to the problem of man lies in Christ.*

BERDYAEV

The history of the world is nothing but the history of the war waged by the powers of the world and of hell since the beginning against the souls humbly devoted to the divine action. In this war the advantages seem all on the side of pride, and yet humility always wins the day. The order of God has always remained victorious; those who have been on His side have triumphed with Him and are happy for eternity; injustice has never been able to protect the deserters . . . The man who has wickedness in his mind always believes himself invincible. But, O God! how can we resist Thee? A single soul with hell and the world against it can fear nothing if it be on the side of surrender to God's order. This monstrous show of impiety armed with so much power; this gold head, this body of silver, bronze and iron is but the phantom of iridescent dust. A tiny pebble scatters it to the winds . . . *How admirable is the Holy Spirit in this dramatic representation of all the ages. So many revolutions which create such havoc among men, such heroes who come in such splendour like so many constellations moving in the sky over our*

*heads; so many wonderful events . . . All who freely
serve iniquity become the slaves of justice, and the
divine action builds the Heavenly Jerusalem with the
ruins of Babylon.*
                              JEAN-PIERRE DE CAUSSADE

What is divine in Man is elusive and impalpable, and
he is easily tempted to embody it in a concrete form –
a church, a country, a social system, a leader – so that
he may realize it with less effort and serve it with more
profit. Yet, as even Lincoln proved, the attempt to
externalize the kingdom of heaven in a temporal shape
must end in disaster. It cannot be created by charters
and constitutions nor established by arms. Those
who set out for it alone will reach it together,
and those who seek it in company will perish by
themselves.
                              HUGH KINGSMILL

The Journalist remembers as a child going for walks with
his father. There might be rough ground, a heavy climb,
marshlands, etc., but he did not worry. He had faith in his
father; he knew that his purpose was loving not malign,
and that he could be counted on to arrive safely back at
home, and to deal with any difficulties which might arise.
In the same way with God, if we have faith there can be
no occasion for fear or anxiety. Fears are the measure of
our lack of faith.

It is precisely when every earthly hope has been explored and found wanting, when every possibility of
help from earthly sources has been sought and is not
forthcoming, when every recourse this world offers,
moral as well as material, has been drawn on and
expended with no effect, when in the shivering cold
every faggot has been thrown on the fire, and in the

gathering darkness every glimmer of light has finally flickered out – it is then that Christ's hand reaches out, sure and firm, that Christ's words bring their inexpressible comfort, that His light shines brightest, abolishing the darkness for ever.

A truly peaceful day from beginning to end is a great rarity in this life.

The Romans made mosaics on the ground, the Christians pointed steeples into the sky.

Unable to find accommodation in Moscow, the Journalist and his wife, K, move to Kliasma, some little distance out of Moscow, where they have been lent a dacha. There, K runs a high temperature, and it turns out that she has some sort of typhus infection. The Journalist remembers this illness in India, and a dreadful fear seizes him that, as a result of his crazy venture in bringing K to the USSR, he may lose her and the child in her womb – for she is pregnant. Now what alone matters to him is to save K and their child, begotten in love and to be born into love; new life clamouring to come into the world, an infinitesimal particle of God's creation with all the potentiality this implies. The Journalist has experienced a love that transcends all its familiar expressions and indulgences and attributes; speechless, as remote from carnal implications as a wager at the Eucharist is remote from gourmandise; giving, maybe, across infinitude a whiff of God's love for His creation, like a tearing east wind carrying intimations of spring.

Lust and Love

A man and a woman were sleeping together in a flat in the Avenue Henri Martin (an absurd chromium flat with a bar and huge mirrors). The man wakes up in the night to hear someone being murdered in the street outside, whose last grunts were curiously like the grunts the man and his companion had been emitting earlier, and it occurred to him that all manifestations of passion are the same. The only escape from passion is through love; its only mitigation procreation.

*

Food is for nourishment, with gastronomy an incidental. Likewise, fornication is for procreation, with eroticism as an incidental. In the same sort of way, Truth is for enlightenment, with meaning an incidental. Change this round, and make gastronomy the end and nourishment the incidental, eroticism the end and procreation the incidental, and sickness ensues – in the one case, satiety, in the other impotence; in both cases, the ultimate outcome is the vomitorium. As for the quest for truth – it gets lost in the quicksand of history, the jungle of fact, the slough of meaning or consensus. To make all this clear to us, God has adopted His usual device of *reductio ad absurdum*, providing so much food that the prevention of obesity becomes a cult, so much and so varied eroticism that desire itself falters and dies, and finally, along comes this computer, the ultimate farce of fact.

The Journalist has to report the anniversary celebrations of the October Revolution. This involves leaving K and the newcomer, ever more active in her womb, and going to Moscow for the occasion. In Red Square the tanks go rattling by; overhead, fighter planes fly past in formation; then come the infantry goose-stepping to perfection – all this to the great joy of foreign pacifists like Henri Barbusse and the Dean of Canterbury, Dr Hewlett Johnson, in full canonicals, not to mention domestic celebrities like Maxim Gorky, who, on his visits to the USSR from his villa in Italy, gets more and more like a performing seal, so practised has he become in doing, saying and being what is expected of him. On top of Lenin's mausoleum the Politbureau are arrayed, Stalin a little to the fore, and bowing in response to the usual orchestrated and monitored applause. The Journalist, like all his colleagues, is on the lookout for absentees; the Soviet bosses only make hard news by disappearing. This time the Politbureau seem to be all present and correct.

Back in Kliasma, the Journalist takes an occasional break from nursing K to stroll among the nearby pine trees. Two scenes occupy his mind – K, in their dacha, fighting for her life and for the life of their child; in Red Square, military might in the shape of tanks and aeroplanes and marching men, and political might in the shape of frightened men clustered together on Lenin's mausoleum, soon to be killed off or otherwise disposed of by their great leader, Stalin. Somehow the two scenes seem related; the Red Square one so enormously more powerful, more significant than the other, which is just a matter of a distended belly enclosing a barely formed body. Yet the Journalist's soul tells him it is the other way round; in Red Square they are but playing at soldiers, whereas in struggling like K to live and bring forth new life, God's creation is being fulfilled – Let there be life! And there was life, and it was good!

The Journalist is so uplifted by this thought that he has an impulse to kneel down then and there and offer thanks, but he refrains, contenting himself with smiling at other walkers among the pine trees, who, unlike the passers-by in Moscow streets, smile back at him – dear brother! dear sister! He makes a point, too, of taking a look at a little deserted church which has fascinated him ever since he moved to Kliasma. Now someone, greatly daring, has touched up its coloured front, formerly faded and neglected, making it shine in the light of the setting sun. So, with great joy and exuberance, the Journalist has a sense that all is well, with life triumphant pushing upwards in the trees and flowers and herbage, and the contrary force – power – pulling downwards with gravity, and between the two the drama of our existence being enacted. In keeping with this mood, on returning to the dacha from his walk the Journalist finds K appreciably better; her temperature has fallen, she wants to eat. Soon she is well enough to go to England, and there the child she has so cherished in her womb is safely delivered – their son John.

On his own in Moscow, the Journalist continues to provide coverage of the Soviet scene, and then decides to make his way to the Ukraine and report on the famine conditions alleged to prevail there. They prove to be even worse than anticipated, and in three articles, dispatched to Manchester via a diplomatic bag, he describes in detail the suffering and privation that has come about as a result of Stalin's insistence on immediate and full scale collectivization of agriculture, and on the purging of the Kulaks, the better-off peasants. He knows that once the articles are published his position in Moscow will become an impossible one, so he prepares to make his departure. Looking back on the scene in the Ukraine, one particular experience stands out above all others:

Sunday in Kiev

On a Sunday morning the Journalist finds himself in the ancient city of Kiev, capital of the Ukraine, and on an impulse turns into a church where a Mass is in progress. The church is packed tight, but he manages to squeeze himself against a pillar where he can survey the congregation and see the altar and the Mass being celebrated. It is a variegated congregation – young and old, peasants and townspeople, parents and children, even a few soldiers in uniform. The bearded priests intoning their prayers and swinging their censers seem very remote and far away. Never before or since has he participated in such worship; the sense conveyed of turning to God in great affliction is overpowering. Though he cannot, of course, follow the service word by word, he grasps its general theme – that now there is no other recourse than to throw ourselves on God's mercy and pray for His help. What intense feeling they put into their prayers and worship! In their minds, he feels sure, as in his, is a picture of desolate abandoned villages, of cattle-trucks being loaded in the dawn light with human bodies to be transported to the Gulag Archipelago, of prevailing hunger and hopelessness. Where are they to turn for help? Not to the Kremlin and the Dictatorship of the Proletariat, certainly; nor to the forces of progress and enlightenment in the West, such as they are. Honourable and Right Honourable Members have nothing to offer; *Gauche Radicale* is unforthcoming; likewise, the *soi-disant* Free Press. Every possible human agency is found wanting. So, only God remains, and to God they turn, with a passion, a dedication, a humility impossible to convey. They take the Journalist with them; he feels closer to God than he ever has before.

> But this I say, brethren, this time is short.
> THE APOSTLE PAUL

We are like people waking from sleep, who cannot collect their thoughts at once, or understand where they are. Little by little the truth breaks upon us. In the present world we are sons of light gradually waking to a knowledge of ourselves. For that let us meditate, let us pray, let us work, gradually to attain a real apprehension of what we are. Thus, as time goes on, little by little we shall give up shadows. Waiting on God day by day we shall make progress day by day, and approach to the true and clear view of what He has made us to be in Christ.

In truth it is very difficult to draw out our reasons for our religious convictions, and that on many accounts. It is very painful to a man of devout mind to do so; for it implies, or even involves, a steadfast and almost curious gaze at God's wonder-working presence within and over him, from which he shrinks, as savouring of a high-minded and critical temper. And much more is it painful, not to say impossible, to put these reasons forth as explicit statements, because they are so very personal and private. Yet, as in order to the relief of his own perplexity, a religious man may at times try to ascertain them, so again for the service of others he will try, as best he may, to state them.

JOHN HENRY NEWMAN

As the Journalist prepares to leave Moscow, he asks himself what he has learnt in his time in the USSR – certainly a drastic and unforgettable experience. His conclusion is that what he has learnt is something very simple and definite: that human beings can never be made brotherly, happy and peaceful by the exercise of power, but only by the experience of love. Jesus's claim to have overcome the world just when the world would seem to have overcome Him – "In the world ye shall have tribulation; but be of good cheer, I have overcome the world" – proves to be well founded, whereas Caesar's conquests, seemingly so widespread and definitive, are fated to fall to the barbarians. Jesus, that is to say, overcomes the world by being overcome; Caesar's triumphs chart the way to his Empire's decline and fall.

The Journalist spends his last evening in Moscow, as he did his first, in walking round and round Red Square. It has not changed, but he has; his preoccupation now is with the fallacy and fantasy of power rather than with its potentialities; with the absurdity of pitting Man's feeble will against God's purposes for His creation, Man's mortality against God's immortality, fallen Man against the risen Christ. This is the revelation that has come to the Journalist as a result of the time he has spent in the USSR. May it stay with him, he prays.

Thus the Journalist for the first time grasps the stupendous truth that superman's victories are all defeats, whereas the crucified Christ is the everlasting victor. In these circumstances, the Journalist asks himself, is he to be counted among the deluded mob who follow the consensus and obediently shout: "Crucify Him! Crucify Him!"? Or should he not rather, as the disciples were instructed, take up his cross and follow the risen Christ?

Such a consideration stirs up inside him a tremendous longing. Yes, that is precisely what he wants – not just to contemplate the possibility of handing over his life to Christ, but doing it then and there, unconditionally, and for ever. Here is my life, such as it is; take it, Lord! This is the very first time that the Journalist has seriously considered the possibility of so total a commitment – turning aside for ever from fleshly and egotistic pursuits; concentrating his attention on the needs of others rather than on his own appetites, on love and his soul rather than on power and his will; living in Eternity rather than Time. The prospect is thrilling, and yet somehow terrifying too. As he turns over in his mind all its different aspects and possibilities his ever-active ego moves in, and he sees himself as a monk in his habit, a Franciscan preferably, sought after by lost souls everywhere, a saint-to-be. Or as an evangelist addressing great gatherings of people who hang on his words. Or as a priest in his vestments popping the Blessed Sacrament into now open mouths at the altar rail. His ruminations are interrupted by a large limousine with outriders and its blinds drawn, driving through the Kremlin gates, which open and close seemingly of themselves. Is there, he wonders, crouching in the back seat, the little man with the waddling walk and the thick black moustache?

The Journalist knows perfectly well that after what he has written about the famine in the Ukraine his visa will be withdrawn and he will have to leave Russia, probably for good and all. Rather to his surprise, this saddens him. Despite the appalling conditions he has seen on his journey to the Caucasus, the countryside as he remembers it still has a singular beauty. Likewise the people; terrorized, impoverished, brainwashed, cut off from the rest of the world as they are, they none the less in some mysterious way seem to be custodians of the future; out of their terrible suffering and privation will come some new revelation, bringing comfort and hope and faith to a battered and bemused world. Dostoevsky, the Journalist remembers, prophesied something of the sort. Almost as though confirming this, he notices a change in the wind blowing against his face. From being icy it is touched with warmth, and even, the Journalist seems to notice, carries some sort of fragrance, a tiny flavour of flowers which have just unfolded their leaves in preparation for the blooms to come. Now the frozen river will thaw and the sun uncover the earth. It is the coming of Spring; thus it has happened a million times before; thus it will happen a million times again. Nothing can prevent this process taking place – the sudden, unheralded coming of Spring.

Thinking of Dostoevsky and his prophetic vision, the Journalist decides to break his journey homewards at Leningrad, and seek out Dostoevsky's grave in the cemetery there. It takes some time to locate the grave; no one will direct him, Dostoevsky being still officially a reactionary counter-revolutionary. The grave, when he finds it, turns out to be neglected and overgrown, but the weather-beaten bust remains recognizable. Standing beside it, he thinks particularly of Dostoevsky's novel *The Devils*, and of how relevant to the contemporary scene is this study of the Liberal Mind personified in the characters of Verkovensky Senior, an old-fashioned romantic and visionary who manages to find a rich lady to look after him, and of his son, Peter, an anarchist and revolutionary out to bring about chaos and destruction on any terms.

Peter Verkovensky's Followers and Plans

The Teacher who laughs with the children at their God and at their cradle is ours already. The barrister who defends an educated murderer by pleading that, being more mentally developed than his victim, he could not help murdering for money, is already one of us. Schoolboys who kill a pheasant for the sake of a thrill are ours. The juries who acquit all criminals without distinction are ours. A public prosecutor who trembles in court because he is not sufficiently progressive, is ours. Administrators, authors – oh, there are lots and lots of us, and they don't know it themselves . . . But one or two generations of vice are absolutely essential now. Monstrous, disgusting vice which turns man into an abject, cowardly, cruel and selfish wreck – that's what we want! And on top of it, a little "fresh blood" to make them get used to it . . .

DOSTOEVSKY

In the light of this concept of Devils, it occurs to the Journalist that he has been seeing an unending procession of them coming to Moscow in the person of intelligentsia full of admiration for Stalin and the Soviet regime. Lawyers deeply impressed by Soviet justice as exemplified by anti-God museums, teachers seeing in Soviet education a vast improvement on their own, and so on.

Now the Journalist finds himself, along with most of his countrymen, if not of mankind, sleepwalking into another war. Outwardly, this is an appalling prospect which must at all costs be evaded; inwardly, he has a secret longing to put on a uniform and disappear into the anonymity of military service – as it were, picking up the threads of the 1914–18 war which ended just when he was about to be conscripted. His efforts to enlist prove futile, however, since journalism turns out to be a reserved occupation. So he has to make do with being drafted into the newly established Ministry of Information. In the evenings he spends his time wandering about in the London blackout. The whores, he notices, are fitted with little lights like bicycles to indicate their whereabouts. War brings darkness, the Devil's Kingdom, contrasting with God's Kingdom of Light. *Fiat lux* into *Fiat nox*.

The Journalist's work at the Ministry of Information is tedious and depressing; in fighting a war a certain excitement may be expected, but in explaining a war, which is what the Ministry is engaged in, there is, in the words of Ecclesiastes "vanity and vexation of spirit". As veterans from the 1914–18 war shake the mothballs out of their uniforms and polish up their Sam Brownes in preparation for the 1939–45 follow-on, so the Ministry furbishes up old slogans about making the world safe for democracy and fit for heroes to live in. By way of escape, the Journalist manages to get himself enlisted as a lance-corporal, unpaid, in Field Security, later to become the Intelligence Corps, and reports for duty at Mychett Hutments, near Aldershot, the depot of the Corps of Military Police. There, he is fitted with an old-style khaki tunic, riding breeches and puttees, thus becoming an authentic soldier. Battle dress will come later, and, he hopes, in due course battles.

Who shall separate us from the love of Christ?
Shall tribulation, or distress, or persectuion, or
famine, or nakedness, or peril, or sword? . . .

Nay, in all these things we are more than
conquerors through Him that loved us.

For I am persuaded, that neither death, nor life,
nor angels, nor principalities, nor powers, nor
things present, nor things to come, nor height, nor
depth, nor any other creature, shall be able to
separate us from the love of God, which is in Christ
Jesus our Lord.

Romans 8:15–39

Beloved, let us love one another: for love is of
God; and everyone that loveth is born of God, and
knoweth God.
He that loveth not knoweth not God; for God is
love.

1 JOHN 4:7–8

Love

Love bade me welcome; yet my soul drew back,
   Conscious of dust and sin.
But quick-eyed Love, observing me grow slack
   From my first entrance in,
Drew nearer to me, sweetly questioning,
   If I lacked anything.
"A guest", I answered, "worthy to be here."
   Love said, "You shall be he."
"I, the unkind, ungrateful? Ah, my dear,
   I cannot look on thee."
Love took my hand, and smiling did reply,
   "Who made the eyes but I?"
"Truth, Lord, but I have marred them; let my shame
   Go where it doth deserve."

> "And know you not", says Love, "who bore the
>   blame?"
> "My dear, then I will serve."
> "You must sit down", says Love, "and taste my
>   meat."
> So I did sit and eat.

GEORGE HERBERT

Intimations of Conversion

As with the Gregorian plain-chant at Solesmes, Simone
Weil was at first conscious only of the aesthetic quality
of Herbert's work: "I used to think that I was merely
saying beautiful verse; but though I did not know it,
the recitation had the effect of a prayer. And it happened that in the autumn of 1938, as I was saying his
poem *Love*, Christ Himself came down, and He took
me." She had always denied the possibility of "a real
contact, from person to person here on earth, between
a human being and God". However, she had felt the
touch of the divine.

Simone Weil, A fellowship in Love by Jacques Cabaud

Thus uplifted, the Soldier asks himself a direct question –
What does he truly believe? Immediately and instinctively,
he starts chanting to himself, as on so many occasions at
Cambridge in his College Chapel, sometimes in the early
morning when he is only half awake, or in the evening
saying the words without their impinging on his mind: "I
believe in God, the Father Almighty, maker of Heaven and
Earth, and in Jesus Christ His only Son, our Lord . . .",
mentally performing the requisite gestures as he proceeds –
bowing his head, crossing himself, kneeling, and concluding

with an assortment of beliefs leading up to "The Resurrection of the body and the life everlasting. Amen".

Does he really believe it all? Or any of it?, he asks
himself. That God made heaven and earth in two separate
undertakings? Or that he, one of Falstaff's Mortal Men,
when he dies will shed his body, a battered old carcass
anyway, and then be resurrected in this same body, and
live for ever? "Lord, I believe", he wants to say, remembering the man in the New Testament (Mark chapter 9, verses
14–24) whose son has a dumb devil tearing him to pieces
and endangering his life. "Can't you help my son and make
him better?", the father asks Jesus, who replies: "If thou
canst believe, all things are possible to him that believes."
Whereupon father and son together, weeping, cry out:
"Lord, I believe; help thou mine unbelief." In the barrack
hut the Soldier, also with tears, echoes their words: "Lord,
I believe; help thou mine unbelief." He has an impulse then
and there to kneel down by his bed and proclaim his faith,
but cowardice steps in, and instead he curses himself for
having lingered in his cot and lost his first place at the
ablutions.

In the ensuing months the war comes alive for the Soldier;
first at Sheerness in the Isle of Sheppey where he witnesses
the arrival of demoralized French troops, fleeing before the
German *Panzers* advancing on Paris; then, when he is
posted to GHQ Home Forces in St Paul's School, Ham-
mersmith, the Blitz gets into full swing. The Soldier is out
for a Sunday afternoon stroll on Camden Hill when he
hears a loud hum in the clear sky, followed by the sound
of ack-ack and bomb explosions. Thenceforth the Blitz is
a nightly occurrence, a sort of real-life *son et lumière*;
the sirens sound, bombs fall, destroying houses and other
buildings indiscriminately, the dead are counted. Watching
from Parliament Hill, it seems to the Soldier as though
London is on fire, with great flames leaping into the sky, a

pall of smoke everywhere, and the sound of falling buildings. The scene stirs up in him a feeling of exaltation, a terrible joy at the sight and sound and smell of so much destruction. How about Buckingham Palace?, he wants to know. Are the Houses of Parliament still standing? And Broadcasting House? The Law Courts? Above all, Fleet Street, that surely must have been a target!

Then it occurs to the Soldier that thus glorying in destruction is to create it – like children throwing stones at the windows of an empty house; strife and wars must go on happening as long as ardour for destruction exists inside him, gaining momentum all the time, as evil alway does. Thus reflecting, the Soldier feels disgusted with himself for having so easily succumbed to exaltation over the slaughter and havoc the Blitz has brought about. Perhaps, he reflects, it might have been better if he had been destroyed himself rather than glorying in the destruction all around him. One or two incendiary bombs, in fact, have fallen quite near him, and might well have finished him off. The scene of confusion, noise and destruction, and his own foolish delight in it, stirs up the longing, always lurking about inside him, consciously or unconsciously, to have done with all worldliness, to shed his old egotistic and carnal self like a snake shedding its skin, and devote himself wholly to serving God's purposes as revealed in the teachings of Jesus Christ, and symbolized by the Cross on which He died. There is a phrase the Soldier owes to St Francis of Assisi that often echoes in his mind, "naked on the naked earth", conveying, as it does, the most blessed of all conditions, so that he is deaf to the siren voices of the flesh and the Ego, stripped of the tawdry devices and desires of his own heart, and can concentrate his will on one single purpose – a closer walk with God.

The visible world still remains without its divine interpretation; Holy Church in her sacraments . . . will remain, even to the end of the world but a symbol of those heavenly facts which fill eternity. Her mysteries are but the expressions in human language of truths to which the human mind is unequal. Thus nature is a parable and scripture an allegory.

JOHN HENRY NEWMAN

History provides the myths, and myths reveal history. Or, put another way, only by studying myths can history be discovered. Men can live without history, but not without myths. In this sense, everything that happens is a parable rather than an event, or series of events; seen through rather than with, the eye, the message is clear. The Fearful Symmetry declares itself. Thus, in trying to construct perfection in their own image, to institute an earthly paradise, men only succeed in underlining their own imperfection; their earthly paradise is seen to be a heavenly hell.

The Jesus of History has become the Christ of Faith, this being the revelation of the Fearful Symmetry which underlies all human experience, all history, every happening, great and small, to us individually or collectively.

Walking with God

Oh! for a closer walk with God,
A calm and heavenly frame;
A light to shine upon the road
That leads me to the Lamb!

Where is the blessedness I knew
When first I saw the Lord?
Where is the soul-refreshing view
Of Jesus and His word?

What peaceful hours I once enjoyed!
How sweet their memory still!
But they have left an aching void,
The world can never fill.

Return, O holy Dove, return,
Sweet messenger of rest;
I hate the sins that made Thee mourn,
And drove thee from my breast.

The dearest idol I have known,
What e'er that idol be,
Help me to tear it from Thy throne,
And worship only Thee.

So shall my walk be close with God,
Calm and serene my frame;
So purer light shall mark the road
That leads me to the Lamb.

WILLIAM COWPER

War is about killing, but the Soldier is still entangled in words, written and spoken. Despairing of getting involved in any bloody battle, with a prospect of killing and being killed, he falls back on the desperate device of going through the motions of killing himself. This happens in a remote part of Africa, Mozambique, then a Portuguese colony and so neutral territory. The Soldier is posted to the British Consulate-General in the capital city, Lourenço Marques, as a bogus Vice-Consul on behalf of MI6, the wartime version of the Secret Service, or SIS (Secret Intelligence Service). His actual business is counter-espionage, which means finding out what the enemy consuls – Wertz, the German and Campini, the Italian – are up to, and, if possible, frustrating them. This involves participating, or seeming to participate, in the squalid night-life of Lourenço Marques; only possible at all with the help of alcohol. Returning one night, rather tipsy, after such a staged debauch, he falls into a state of unutterable melancholy. Of all the roles he might have envisaged as a belligerent in a war, this one surely would have seemed the most remote – in a faraway part of Africa, near the equator, lurching in and out of night clubs patronized mainly by loud-voiced South Africans out on a spree.

This is the lowest point in the Soldier's life; it is also the most decisive.

He drove to the furthest point along the coast road, some six miles from Lourenço Marques, and there got out of the car and undressed. The lights were still on in Peter's Café and Costa da Sol. As the tide was far out, he had to wade on and on before there was enough water to swim in. So this was the end of his life, his last little while on earth. He kept on trying to think of the French word for "drown". Everything seemed to him unreal – had there been a single moment in his life when he had truly lived? Everything false – love, hate, despair, all equally false. Even his dying seemed false. Was it him, wading on to the open sea? Was it really happening? The bottom he trod on was muddy now, the water creeping up and cold, the air damp. At last there was enough water to swim in. He started swimming, the dark water churning white as his arms beat through it. Soon he was out his depth, and still swam on. Now he felt easy, now it was settled. Looking back he could scarcely see the shore; only the lights of Peter's Café and Costa da Sol, far, far, away. He began to tremble, all his body trembled; he went under the water, trembling, came up again and reposed himself as though on a bed. He could sleep on this watery mattress, sleep. Then, suddenly, without thinking or deciding, he started swimming back to shore. He was very tired, and kept feeling as if he was in his depth again, and wasn't; he shouted foolishly for help, and kept his eyes fixed on the lights of Peter's Café and Costa da Sol.

They were lights of the world; they were the lights of his home, his habitat, where he belonged. He must reach them. There followed an overwhelming joy such as he had never experienced before; an ecstasy. *In some mysterious way it became clear to him that there was no darkness, only the possibility of losing sight of a light which shone eternally;* that our clumsy appetites are no more than the blind reaching of a newly born child after the teat through which to suck the milk of life; that our sufferings, our affliction, are part of a drama – an essential, even an ecstatic, part – endlessly revolving round the two great propositions of good and evil, of light and darkness. A brief interlude, an incarnation, reaching back into the beginning of time, and forward into an ultimate fulfilment in the universal spirit of love which informs, animates, illuminates all creation, from the tiniest particle of insentient matter to the radiance of God's very throne.

Now he felt the bottom, and began to wade labori-ously back to the shore, reaching it by the estuary of a river, a long way away from where he had first gone into the sea. All round him was deep black mud, through which, shaking with cold, he floundered until, by luck more than any sense of direction, he saw his car where he had left it. Even at the time he realized, and realizes now ever more clearly, that this flounder-ing was a sort of parable. Plodding and floundering on through deep mud, but never again without hope;

thenceforth always knowing, deep in his heart, remembering even when he forgot, that it was not by chance or for nothing that the lights of Peter's Café and Costa da Sol had called him back. That he, too, had something he must try to say and be, until the time came for God to put him to sleep, as he had tried, in his own fatuous and sinful wilfulness, to put himself to sleep in the sea off Lourenço Marques. When, finally, he reached his car and clothes, the morning was just breaking; the black African sky just beginning to be tinged with grey. He breathed in the dawn air, greedily; after all, he was still alive.

Though he scarcely realized it at the time, and subsequently only very slowly and dimly, this episode represented for him one of those deep changes which take place in our lives . . . A kind of spiritual adolescence, whereby, thenceforth, all his values and pursuits and hopes were going to undergo a total transformation – from the carnal towards the spiritual; from the immediate, the now, towards the everlasting, the eternal. In a tiny dark dungeon of the ego, chained and manacled, he had glimpsed a glimmer of light coming in through the barred window high above him. It was the light of Peter's Café and Costa da Sol calling him back to earth, his mortal home; it was the grey light of morning heralding another day as he floundered and struggled through the black mud; it was the light of the world. The bars of the window, as he looked more closely, took on the form of a Cross.

Chronicles of Wasted Time

Subsequently, the Soldier often calls to mind the scene of his return to life, and how what summoned him back was not the memory of some past ecstasy – the sound of music carrying him up to immeasurable heights, the overflow of love when two souls melt into one, the glory of a summer's day, the discovery of words reaching beyond their meaning, his children and then grandchildren growing up to follow the everlasting pilgrimage, to whose end he draws near. None of these things called him back, but just the lights of a sleazy café looking over the sea; a noisy haunt of mortal men and women; St Teresa of Avila's second-class hotel.

It dawns on him then that the true wonder of life is indeed its ordinariness rather than an imaginary extra-ordinariness. God did not come among us trailing clouds of glory; incarnate, He was no great scholar, perhaps barely literate, finding that children understand better what He is getting at than do grown-ups, and so addressing Himself to children as being a more worthwhile audience than scribes and Pharisees; consorting for the most part with lowly people, looking for His disciples among fishermen, and even then, one of the chosen twelve proves to be a crook, and the rest ran away.

In any case, God who is infinite cannot be seen by finite eyes or understood by a finite mind. However many millennia our human race may go on existing, this will still be the case; the Cloud of Unknowing that lies between Time and Eternity, between Man and his Creator, can never be pierced. We strain our eyes trying to see God, our ears to hear Him, our minds to understand Him, but all in vain. The mystery is for ever; those who purport to have fathomed it – gurus, miscellaneous *exaltés*, speakers with tongues, scientists, soothsayers – only enhance the mystery. The Cloud of Unknowing remains opaque and impene-trable; clearly, God intends it so. And if and when our eyes are opened, and we understand at last what is the true significance of our brief existence on our little earth, past efforts to explain it, whether scientific (Darwin), ideological (Marx), visionary (William Morris), philosophical (Herbert

Spencer), theological (Bultmann), will seem of little or no significance.

The Soldier spends the rest of the war as a liaison officer with the French *Securité Militaire*, first in North Africa, then in Paris, whose *soi disant* Liberation he witnesses. The Liberation scene, he finds, is not an edifying one; *Èpuration* is the order of the day, with, roughly speaking, everyone informing on everyone else. The police stations overflow with accusations of collaboration, the senders no doubt calculating that the more ferociously they denounce others, the less likely are they to be found guilty themselves. The simple fact is, of course, that everyone who does not make off or go underground when a successful enemy invasion has taken place, will sooner or later find him- or herself collaborating. French shopkeepers will necessarily sell their goods to German soldiers; likewise, French whores sleep with German officers if they happen to attract the attention of one of them; otherwise, with German Other Ranks (ORs). Parisian restaurants are crowded with hungry Germans of all categories, wanting to taste the famous French cuisine; hairdressers run their clippers over bullet-heads from Prussia, and comedians angle their performances so as not to upset German, or even Nazi, sensitivities.

Come the Liberation, and all this changes; German officers have made off post haste, and any ORs who have lingered on soon find that it behoves them to disappear, the sooner the better. The prisons are crowded to overflowing with alleged collaborators, and the courts, mostly manned by former Pétainists, demonstrate their loyalty to the new regime under General de Gaulle by working round the clock at sentencing collaborators to terms of imprisonment or worse.

In the famous restaurant, Maxim's, American and British officers celebrate Liberation without the inconvenience of having to pay a bill. Mme Chanel successfully wards off

Èpuration by putting in the window of her shop an announcement that her famous Chanel No 5 is *gratuit* for
GIs. Fresnes and other prisons are full to overflowing, with
enough politicians to form a government, and enough
actors, actresses and entertainers to keep a non-stop show
with an all-star cast going indefinitely. On the Left Bank it
is business as usual; the red lights shine, the gamblers lay
their bets, and the croupiers rake them in; the stripteasers
throw off their clothes, and the transvestites put them on.
For the Soldier, one face stands out unforgettably – the
large, melancholy countenance of a clown who concludes
his comic tale of woe with shaking his head and muttering
almost as though he was sobbing: "*Et maintenant nous
sommes liberés!*" – "And now we are liberated." The face
of this clown continues to haunt the Soldier; he feels
sure that he has seen it somewhere before. The next day,
catching a glimpse of General de Gaulle, who has just
arrived in Paris, and, without any authority, at once becomes the Government, he realizes at once that the resem-
blance lies with de Gaulle – the same vague melancholy,
the same lost look, the same impression of sleepwalking.
The clown's patter and the General's rhetoric are versions
of the same harlequinade.

As the war draws to its close, the Soldier, with nothing
much else to do in Paris except wait for his discharge, asks
himself: Who, in fact, are the beneficiaries? Who have been
Liberated? Not, certainly, the Berliners in their flattened
city. Nor the people of the countries of East and Central
Europe ostensibly Liberated by the Red Army, which will
stay with them for years to come. Neither the victors nor
the defeated would seem to have been Liberated, individually or collectively; neither those who delivered the atomic
bomb to Hiroshima and Nagasaki, nor those who received
it there, of whom a large number were obliterated. In Paris,
however, the Soldier comes by chance across one person at

least who can be said to have been Liberated. This is a
young woman – call her Françoise – whose parents bring
her to see him. At first glance, she is rather frightening, for
her head has been shaved, making her face seem like a
grotesque mask which has nothing to do with the rest of
her body. Her parents explain what has happened; during
the occupation they have a German soldier billeted upon
them. He turns out to be a friendly soul who helps them
with food and fuel supplies. Almost inevitably, he and
Françoise fell in love with one another. Then comes the
crux of the story; with some shrugging of shoulders and
spreading of hands, it is explained that, as is the way
nowadays, Françoise became *enceinte*.

When the German troops retreat from Paris, Françoise's
lover stays behind to be near her, but the FFI (*Force
Françaises Interieures*) seek him out, and, turning themselves into an execution squad, shoot him down, so that
Françoise is a widow before she is a wife or a mother. This
does not save her from having her head shaved and being
marched through the streets of Paris as an object lesson in
what happens to traitresses. For Françoise the situation is
made the more tragic because there is reason to suppose
that her brother, who joined the FFI, was one of the
executioners. What is remarkable is that her love for her
lost lover, and joy in the child she will bear him, swallows
up her suffering and grief. That is to say, she is Liberated;
she the collaborator, the traitress, in a city *en fête* for its
own *soi disant* Liberation.

As it happens, the Soldier, is able to protect her from any
further attention by the Liberation celebrants. Thereafter he
loses touch with her and her family, but the story of her
Liberation remains with him, linked, as it is, with another
great Liberation occasion – on Golgotha, when a Man is
ridiculed and crucified, thereby demonstrating through the
subsequent twenty centuries that the only way to be truly

Liberated is through suffering and the dynamic of love rather than through exaltation and the dynamic of power. How extraordinary, he reflects, that a woman with a shaved head and a broken heart should point the way to deliverance from servitude to the Ego and the flesh into which we are all born.

Thus the Soldier begins to understand – that there is no Liberation to be achieved through the exercise of power. Armies cannot Liberate, nor is Liberation to be found in the victor's camp. The prisoner finds freedom in the acceptance of his captivity; his gaolers incarcerate themselves. Which is real, the Soldier asks himself, the victory procession down the Champs-Élysées led by Churchill and de Gaulle, or the girl with the shaved head mourning for her lost lover? Like Pilate when he asks what is truth, the Soldier does not wait for an answer.

The shadow of the world falls across the face of innocence.

*   *   *

It was granted me to carry away from my prison years on my bent back, which nearly broke beneath its load, the essential experience: *how* a human being becomes *evil* and how *good*. In the intoxication of my youthful successes I had felt myself to be infallible, and I was therefore cruel. In the surfeit of power I was a murderer, and an oppressor. In my most evil moments I was convinced that I was doing good, and I was well supplied with systematic arguments. And it was only when, in the Gulag Archipelago, on rotting prison straw that I sensed within myself the first stirrings of good. Gradually it was disclosed to me that the line separating good and evil passes, not through states, nor between classes, nor between political parties either –

but right through every human heart and through all human hearts . . . And that is why I turn back to the years of my imprisonment and say, sometimes to the astonishment of those about me: "*Bless you, prison!*"

ALEXANDER SOLZHENITSYN

Come unto me, all ye that labour and are heavy laden, and I will give you rest. Take my yoke upon you and learn of me; for I am meek and lowly in heart; and ye shall find rest unto your souls. For my yoke is easy, and my burden is light.

Matthew 11:28–30

So let us throw away the Ego – a great weight – and the foul-smelling appetites, all the devil's cargo, and lo! the ship sails merrily away. Likewise, the Gadarene madman is delivered from his furies, all transferred to a flock of swine who then leap furiously into the sea. The prisoner is released from his bondage to his sins; the ropes that bind him to his cupidity and carnality fall away, and he gathers into the Apostle Paul's glorious liberty of the children of God, compared with which no other liberty has any significance or existence.

*   *   *

The sacrifices of God are a borken spirit: a broken and contrite heart, O God, thou wilt not despise.

9

The Foreign
Correspondent

Having made up his mind that, after all, Paris has *not* been
Liberated, the Soldier decides to Liberate himself by putting
on civilian clothes and joining his wife and children; this
without any further consultation with his superior officers.
Also, he manages to get a job on the *Daily Telegraph*. Then
recurs the same old ritual – sitting round the editor's desk
and considering what subjects might lend themselves to
editorial attention. The available space is so small owing
to paper rationing that somehow the pomposity of the
words used seems particularly ridiculous – like an astra-
khan collar on a tattered old overcoat. In London the
scars of war are still in evidence: weeds growing on the
bombsites, and pools of water collecting there when it
rains. The interior of an occasional bombed building, with
wallpaper, fireplace, mantelpiece, still exposed to view; as
it might be a discarded set in a film studio. Also, the bombed
churches, looking like archaeological ruins, which some of
them, never to be restored, will remain, reduced by the
Blitz to this condition in the twinkling of an eye instead of
quietly decomposing through the passing years. Here and
there, too, forgotten sandbags piled up, and tattered posters
still on display warning that careless talk costs lives. As
for the passers-by, some are still in uniform, some with
fragments of uniforms about their person – a battle-dress

tunic, a belt, a British warm; this worn by the sometime Soldier, but without badges of rank.

In these circumstances, the old urge to be gone makes itself felt. Very conveniently, he hears that the *Daily Telegraph* correspondent in Washington, D. C., wants to move, and offers himself as a replacement. Then and there the matter is settled, and with mixed feelings of exhilaration and despair he makes the necessary arrangements. K comes to see him off at Liverpool. As his ship moves away he sees her on the quay waving to him, and getting smaller and smaller as the distance between them lengthens, until at last she is out of sight. Then anguish seizes him. What is he doing, he asks himself, but filling in time? Bored here, he must go there; tired of such a person, he must cultivate some other person. So his life has no real meaning, is all spent wandering about the world, only to find that its variety is an illusion; that everywhere, everyone and everything endlessly recur. Once again the awful temptation presents itself; so easy this time to slip over the side of the ship and into the sea with no Costa da Sol to call him back, no wading through shallow water on to dry land. Now he is leaning over the ship's side, and watching the wake it leaves behind. No one around to watch him go over; no chance of the body being found, no residuum at all except a few lines in the *Daily Telegraph* on the strange disappearance of its lately appointed Washington Correspondent, with no mention of a broken heart, then or ever.

Why should he thus be dogged by the notion of obliterating himself? He recalls Tolstoy's description of how he has to hide away a rope lying about in his room for fear of using it to hang himself – Tolstoy, a great writer, famous, rich, with a wife and children whom he loves, a beautiful home, Yasnaya Polyana. The Correspondent, too, with a loving and beloved wife, and delightful children, has every reason to be well content with his life, and to want to go on living. Yet every now and again the dark clouds gather; and *accidie* takes possession of him.

Lying in his bunk and conscious of the ship's swell, but not too conscious, a phrase out of the Book of Common Prayer comes into the Correspondent's mind with great insistence – "Whose service is perfect freedom". How wonderful it would be, to pick up his cross, with no other consideration than following Him wherever He might lead, in the certainty that in so doing he would experience as never before perfect freedom. What inexpressible joy! No matter if he was led to Golgotha in the role of a third miscreant to be crucified beside Jesus, it would still be a wonderful deliverance from ambition, greed, envy, lust, into the glorious liberty of God's children. Then the gong for dinner sounds, and the Correspondent breaks off his ruminations to look for a pretty face among his fellow travellers, and in the expectation that a place has been allotted to him at the Captain's table as a person of distinction and importance.

Having arrived in Washington, D. C., and sitting in his little office in the National Press Building, the Correspondent tries to keep abreast of the two ticker-tapes ticking away there, and spilling out quantities of yellow paper covered with news which piles up on the floor, to the point that if the Correspondent happens to be away for a while, when he returns the office door will scarcely open. From time to time he bends down and gathers up a handful or two of news to see whether there is any item liable to be of interest to readers of the *Daily Telegraph* on their daily journey from the Home Counties to London City. There are also on his desk the daily newspapers piled high, on Sundays reaching elephantine proportions, but also, like the ticker tape, containing little nuggets of news which can be sifted out and dispatched across the Atlantic. No need really to look elsewhere; one of the Correspondent's fellow-journalists has his ticker tape machine in his apartment, and keeps up an excellent coverage without ever going out, except for very special occasions. Otherwise, telephone calls suffice. In the morning when he wakes up he delves into the night's accumulation, and before going to bed he takes one last lingering look at what the day has brought forth. The Correspondent often thinks of him in his dressing gown, like some old hermit looking after a shrine; in his case, dedicated to News Everlasting. – "In the beginning was the News, and the news became words, and dwelt among us, graceless and full of lies."

The greater part of the Correspondent's time is spent in an unending quest for news. In addition to the ticker tapes and the day's papers, there are other sources. For instance, up on Capitol Hill, the Senate and the House of Representatives conduct their business, and the Correspondent has a special press pass enabling him to listen to their proceedings, often decidedly turgid, especially the Senators, who are provided with spitoons into which they spit from time to time. There is also the State Department where Dean Acheson and General Marshall preside. Then, as a very long shot, a call at the British Embassy in Massachusetts Avenue, in the unlikely event that someone up there will have something to say about something.

Finally, the biggest deal of all, there is the President's Press Conference in the White House, at which all the journalists from home and abroad gather round the President – in this case, Harry S. Truman – seated at his desk in the Oval Room. The Correspondent studies him carefully – very neatly turned out, blue serge suit, two points of a handkerchief projecting from his breast pocket, trousers carefully pressed, shoes shining. First, the President takes up some sheets of paper and begins to read a communiqué on the Atomic Bomb; like a schoolmaster giving a dictation, his face quite expressionless, the words carefully enunciated. Then come questions – Mr President this, Mr President that. He answers as best he can, only once or twice falling back on: "No comment!" Then it is over; the news agency men run for all they are worth to the telephones – one of them so doing on a previous occasion breaks his leg. This time, safe and sound, they get their stories off ahead of the others.

By the time the Correspondent is back in his office the ticker tape is already disgorging its own version of the President's Press Conference, having, as it were, dished up what was said in the Oval Room with suitable condiments and then baked it in a quick oven. Further experience of news gathering in Washington, D. C. makes the Correspondent increasingly aware of the mystery of the world's happenings and of those who purport to shape them. Moreover, as the means of collecting and transmitting news accelerates, so that words, and later images, flash across the world like lightning, the authenticity of news becomes ever more dubious in the eyes of those who handle it, and ever more convincing in the eyes of those to whom it is served up.

Following on from this thought, the Correspondent goes on to reflect that, likewise, what is transcendental in our mortal existence remains a mystery, to be believed in through faith rather than explored through facts – *credo* rather than *scio*. Indeed, facts, he decides, have come to be the great will-o'-the-wisp of our time. A book on this theme that the Correspondent comes to cherish above all others is *The Cloud of Unknowing*, thought to be by a fourteenth-century monk whose rough piety and splendidly blunt truthfulness gives his narrative a special piquancy. Enlightenment, he tells us, comes rather from accepting a mystery than from attempts to unravel it. It is the Cloud of Knowing that brings down the darkness. Blake, with amazing prescience, showed his awareness of this when he scribbled across Francis Bacon's *Advancement of Learning*, a classic of the Enlightenment: "Good news for Satan's Kingdom."

The Cloud of Unknowing

Look now forwards and let the backwards be.

*

Between us and our God there is not a Cloud of Air but a Cloud of Unknowing.

*

Of God Himself can no man think . . . He may well be loved but not thought. By love may He be gotten and holden, but by thought neither.

*

Beat evermore on this Cloud of Unknowing that is betwixt thee and thy God with a sharp dart of longing love.

*

My blabbering fleshly tongue . . . The great rust of sin.

*

Lesson, Meditation and Orison . . . Otherwise, Reading, Thinking and Praying.

*

Let be this everywhere and this aught in comparison of this nowhere and this naught, which are nothing else than the divine Cloud of Unknowing.

*

The most godly knowing of God is that which is known by unknowing.

*

For not what thou art, nor what thou hast been doth God regard with His merciful eyes, but what thou would'st be.

*

Now truly I trow that who so will not go the strait way to Heaven, they shall go the soft way to Hell.

*

Unless it be restrained by this light of grace in the reason, it will never cease, sleeping or waking, to portray diverse disordered images of bodily creatures; or else some fantasy, the which is naught else but a bodily conceit of a ghostly thing, or else a ghostly conceit of a bodily thing. And this evermore feigned and false.

*

And because that ever the whiles thou livest in this wretched life, thou must always feel in some part this foul stinking lump of sin, as it were oned and congealed with the substance of thy being; therefore shalt thou alternately mean these two words – SIN and GOD. With this general understanding; that if thou hadst God, then shouldst thou lack sin; and mightest thou lack sin, then shouldst thou have God . . . For I tell thee truly, that the devil hath his contemplatives as God hath His.

In his new circumstances the Correspondent becomes more than ever preoccupied with the thought of his own sins, which clutter up his life like seaweed in the Saragossa Sea. As for the Devil – who can fail to admire his cleverness in putting it around that he does not exist, thereby acquiring a completely free hand in fulfilling his own diabolical purposes? Personally, the Correspondent knows beyond a shadow of doubt that in fact the Devil *does* exist, for he has seen his unmistakable face in a mirror – flushed, greedy, the eyes misted over; altogether a study in carnality. It comes as a terrible shock to him when, on closer examination, he recognizes the face in the mirror as his own. Then he wants to shout out as Bunyan's Pilgrim did while still borne down with his burden of sin: "O wretched man that I am! Who shall deliver me from the body of this death?" In the Correspondent's case, the heaviest item in his burden of sin is lechery, with its fraudulent ecstasy, its simulated protestations of love and dreadful confusion of lust and love.

*   *   *

In trying to cope with what St Augustine calls "scratching the itching sore of his lust", the Correspondent finds both solace and elucidation in Augustine's *Confessions*, which describe with great clarity and force, first his surrender to egotistic and erotic impulses, then the struggle to disengage from the downward pull of appetites and the will, and to reach upwards towards the ineffable truth Augustine and his mother, Monica, glimpsed together in Ostia shortly before she died:

> The tumults of the flesh were hushed, hushed the images of earth, and waters, and air; hushed also the poles of Heaven, yes the very soul hushed to herself, and by not thinking of self surmounting self, hushed all dreams and imaginary revelations, every tongue and every sign, and whatsoever only exists in transition . . . And God alone speaks, not through any tongue of flesh, nor Angel's voice, nor sound of thunder, nor in the dark riddle of a similitude, that we might hear His Very Voice.
>
> ST AUGUSTINE

It is in A.D. 410, in Carthage in North Africa, that Augustine hears the desolating news that Rome has been sacked. If the days of the great Roman Empire are indeed over, he tells his flock, it is only what has happened sooner or later to every earthly kingdom. They must not lose heart; the world has grown old and is full of pressing tribulation, the world as they know it is passing away ... Here truly, he says, we have no continuing city, but still we look for one; the cities that men build they sooner or later destroy, but there is also the City of God, which men did not build, and which they cannot destroy. Augustine is indeed fated to see the western Roman Empire well on the way to its end.

The Correspondent ventures to trace a certain parallelism between his own career and Augustine's, both of them being, in Augustine's phrase, "vendors of words"; fugitives from mortality without losing their appreciation of the beauties the world offers; the delights of human love; and above all the joy and fulfilment of reaching out to God, their Creator via the Incarnation. In a famous passage in Book 10 of the *Confessions* Augustine asks himself what he loves when he loves God, and concludes that though his love for God transcends earthly loves, it yet partakes of them:

> But what do I love, when I love Thee? not beauty of bodies, nor the fair harmony of time, nor the brightness of the light, so gladsome to our eyes, nor sweet melodies of varied songs, nor the fragrant smell of flowers, and ointments, and spices, not manna and honey, not limbs acceptable to embracements of flesh. None of these I love, when I love my God; and yet I love a kind of light, and melody, and fragrance, and embracement, when I love my God, the light, melody, fragrance, embracement of my inner man: where there shineth unto my soul what space cannot contain, and there soundeth, what time beareth not away, and there smelleth, what breathing disperseth not, and there tasteth, what eating diminisheth not, and there clingeth, what satiety divorceth not. This is it I love, when I love my God.

It is Augustine's splendid destiny to offer the alternative reality of Christ to a bored, sick, decomposing world of fantasy; to go on to the very end proclaiming in the shambles of the once great Roman Empire the everlasting glory and availability of the City of God. What a wonderful example of what Blake calls Fearful Symmetry, that some twenty centuries later a tawdry presentation of the obscenities of the Emperor Claudius on a television screen provides a diversion for another decomposing world of fantasy. Some future Gibbon will surely note that in the last twilight of Christendom the advanced technology then available is used to bring in the decadence of the old world to complete the decadence of the new.

St Augustine's Confessions

Entrust the past to God's mercy, the present to His love and the future to His providence.

*

Man is a great depth, O Lord; You number his hairs, but the hairs of his head are easier by far to count than his feelings, the movements of his heart.

*

We take for granted the slow miracles whereby year by year water irrigating a vineyard becomes wine, we stand amazed when the same process takes place in quick motion in Cana of Galilee.

*

I am ashamed that my tongue cannot live up to my heart.

*

Men go to gape at mountain peaks, at the boundless tides of the sea, the broad sweep of rivers, the encircling ocean and the motions of the stars, and yet they leave themselves unnoticed; they do not marvel at themselves.

*

Is there any more marvellous sight, any occasion when human reason is nearer to some sort of converse with the nature of things, than the sowing of seeds, the planting of cuttings, the transplantation of shrubs, the grafting of slips?

*

I could not find myself; how much less, then, could I find God.

*

There is a light unchangeable, seen with the eye of the soul. He that knows the truth knows what that light is, and he that knows it, knows Eternity.

*

O greedy men, what will satisfy you if God Himself will not?

*

Now let us hear, brothers, let us hear and sing; let us pine for the City where we are citizens. By pining we are already there; we have already cast our hope, like an anchor on that coast.

10

A Spiritual Pilgrimage

In the course of filming "The Holy Land", during which I saw the reality of Jesus's wilderness, the desert, I visited the Church of the Nativity in Bethlehem. And it was here that I received the first intimation of conversion – a mystical feeling, a sense of being someone else and of some other way of life not connected with the ego's pursuits. I may have been on the stage of the Holy Land, but the play was Jesus Himself.

I remember the precise moment of illumination. I was sitting in the crypt waiting for the time when the public was excluded and we could begin to film. Earlier in the day we had been filming in nearby fields where, reputedly, shepherds were tending their flocks when they heard the tidings of great joy. Sure enough, in the fields there was a shepherd with his flock – sheep and goats duly separated, just as required. When he caught sight of us and our equipment he picked up one of his sheep in his arms, precisely as in the coloured pictures I remembered so well from scripture lessons in my childhood. Then, when he had established his posture, and our cameraman was focusing for a shot, he put down the sheep and came forward to haggle over his fee.

It was after settling this unseemly transaction, and getting our footage of the shepherd and his flock, that we went into the Church of the Nativity, having the greatest difficulty in making our way because of the press of beggars and children offering picture postcards, rosaries and other souvenirs for sale.

I had found a seat in the crypt on a stone ledge in the shadow cast by the lighted candles which provided the only illumination. How ridiculous these so-called "shrines" were!, I was thinking to myself. How squalid the commercialism which exploited them! Who but a credulous fool could possibly suppose that the place marked in the crypt with a silver cross was veritably the spot where Jesus had been born? The Holy Land, it seemed to me, had been turned into a sort of Jesusland, on the lines of Disneyland.

As these thoughts passed through my mind, I began to notice the demeanour of the visitors coming into the crypt. Some crossed themselves; a few knelt down; most were obviously standard twentieth-century pursuers of happiness for whom the Church of the Nativity was just an item in a sightseeing tour – as it might be the Taj Mahal, or Madame Tussaud's, or Lenin's mausoleum.

None the less, each face as it came into view was in some degree transfigured by the experience of being in what purported to be the actual scene of Jesus's birth. This was where it happened, they all seemed to be saying. Here He came into the world! Here we shall find Him! The boredom, the idle curiosity, the vagrant thinking all disappeared. Once more in that place glory shone around, and angel voices proclaimed: *Unto you is born this day . . . a Saviour, which is Christ the Lord!*, thereby transforming it from a tourist attraction into an authentic shrine.

Where two or three are gathered together in my name, Jesus promised, **there I am in the midst of them.** The promise has been kept even in the unlikeliest of places – His own ostensible birthplace.

It is written in the Old Testament that no man may see God and live; at the same time, as Kierkegaard points out, God cannot make man His equal without transforming

him into something more than man. The only solution
was for God to become man, which He did through the
Incarnation in the person of Jesus. Thereby He set a window
in the tiny dark dungeon of the ego in which we all languish,
letting in a light, providing a vista, and offering a way of
release from the servitude of the flesh and the fury of the
will into what St Paul called "the glorious liberty of the
children of God".

This is what the Incarnation, realized in the birth of
Jesus, and in the drama of His ministry, death and resurrection, was to signify. With it Eternity steps into Time, and
Time loses itself in Eternity. Hence Jesus; in the eyes of
God, a Man, and, in the eyes of men, a God. It is sublimely
simple; a transcendental soap opera going on century after
century in which there have been endless variations in the
script, in the music, in the dialogue, but in which one thing
remains constant – the central figure, Jesus.

It was padding about the streets of Moscow that the
other dream – the kingdom of heaven on earth – dissolved
for me, never to be revived. Those grey, anonymous figures,
likewise padding about the streets, seemed infinitely remote, withdrawn, forever strangers, yet somehow near and
dear. The grey streets were paradise, the eyeless buildings
the many mansions of which heaven is composed. I caught
another glimpse of paradise in Berlin after it had been
"Liberated" – there the mansions made of rubble, and the
heavenly hosts, the glow of "Liberation" still upon them,
bartering cigarettes for tins of Spam, and love for both.
(Later, this paradise was transformed by means of mirrors
into a shining, glowing one, running with *Schlag* and fat
cigars, with bartered love still plentifully available, but for
paper money, not Spam.) So many paradises springing up
all over the place, all with many mansions, mansions of
light and love; the most majestic of all, the master paradise
on which all the others were based – on Manhattan Island!

Oh, what marvellous mansions there reaching into the sky! What heavenly Musak overflowing the streets and buildings, what brilliant lights spelling out what delectable hopes and desires, what heavenly hosts pursuing what happiness on magic screens in living colour!

And You, Jesus? I never caught even a glimpse of You in any paradise – unless You were an old, coloured shoeshine man on a windy corner in Chicago one February morning, smiling from ear to ear; or a little man with a lame leg in the Immigration Department in New York, whose smiling patience as he listened to one Puerto Rican after another seemed to reach from there to eternity. Oh, and whoever painted the front of the little church in the woods at Kliasma near Moscow – painted it in blues as bright as the sky and whites that outshone the snow? That might have been You. Or again at Kiev, at an Easter service when the collectivization famine was in full swing, while Bernard Shaw and newspaper correspondents were telling the world of the bursting granaries and apple-cheeked dairymaids in the Ukraine. What a congregation that was, packed in tight, squeezed together like sardines! I myself was pressed against a stone pillar, and scarcely able to breathe. Not that I wanted to, particularly. So many grey, hungry faces, all luminous like an El Greco painting; and all singing. How they sang – about how there was no help except in You, nowhere to turn except to You; nothing, nothing that could possibly bring any comfort except You. I could have touched You then, You were so near – not up at the altar, of course, where the bearded priests, crowned and bowing and chanting, swung their censers – one of the grey faces, the greyest and most luminous of all.

It was strange in a way that I should thus have found myself nearest to You, Jesus, in the land where for half a century past the practice of the Christian religion has been most ruthlessly suppressed; where the very printing of the

Gospels is forbidden, and You are derided by all the organs of an all-powerful state as once You were by ribald Roman soldiers when they decked You out as King of the Jews. Yet, on reflection, not so strange. How infinitely preferable it is to be abhorred, rather than embraced, by those in authority. Where the distinction between God and Caesar is so abundantly clear, no one in his senses – or out of them, for that matter – is likely to suggest that any good purpose would be served by arranging a dialogue between the two of them. In the Communist countries an unmistakable and unabridgeable abyss divides the kingdoms on earth in the Devil's gift and Your kingdom, with no crazed clerics gibbering and grimacing in the intervening no man's land. It provides the perfect circumstances for the Christian faith to bloom anew – so uncannily like the circumstances in which it first bloomed at the beginning of the Christian era. I look Eastwards, not Westwards, for a new Star of Bethlehem.

It would be comforting to be able to say, Now I see! To recite with total satisfaction one of the Church's venerable creeds: "I believe in God, the Father Almighty . . ." To point to such a moment of illumination when all became miraculously clear. To join with full identification in one of the varieties of Christian worship. Above all, to feel able to say to You, "Lord!" and confidently await Your command. Comforting – but, alas, it would not be true. The one thing above all others that You require of us is, surely, the Truth. I have to confess, then, that I can only fitfully believe, can believe no creed wholly, have had no all-sufficing moment of illumination.

And You? What do I know of You? A living presence in the world; the One who, of all the billions of the human family came most immediately from God and went most immediately to God, while remaining most humanly and intimately here among us, today, as yesterday and tomorrow; for all time. Did You live and die and rise from the dead as they say? Who knows, or, for that matter, cares? History is for the dead, and You are alive. Similarly, all those churches raised and maintained in Your name, from the tiniest, weirdest conventicle to the great cathedrals rising so sublimely into the sky – they are for the dead, and must themselves die; are, indeed, dying fast. They belong to time, You to eternity. At the intersection of time and eternity – nailed there – You confront us; a perpetual reminder that living, we die, and dying, we live. An incarnation wonderful to contemplate; the light of the world, indeed.

Fiat lux! Let there be light! So everything began at God's majestic command; so it might have continued till the end of time – history unending – except that You intervened, shining another light into the innermost recesses of the human will, where the ego reigns and reaches out in tentacles of dark desire. Having seen this other light, I turn to it, striving and growing towards it as plants do towards the sun, the light of love, abolishing the darkness of strife and confusion; the light of life, abolishing the darkness of death; the light of creativity, abolishing the darkness of destruction. Though, in terms of history, the darkness falls, blacking out us and our world, You have overcome history. You came as light into the world in order that whoever believed in You should not remain in darkness. Your light shines in the darkness, and the darkness has not overcome it. Nor ever will.

I have always felt myself to be a stranger here on earth, aware that our home is elsewhere. Now, nearing the end of my pilgrimage, I have found a resting place in the Catholic Church from where I can see the Heavenly Gates built into Jerusalem's Wall more clearly than from anywhere else, albeit if only through a glass darkly.

Father Bidone, an Italian priest, now alas dead, and

Mother Teresa have been the major influence in my final decision to join the Catholic Church, although it took me a long time to do so.

I rejoiced over the award of the Nobel Peace Prize to Mother Teresa. Not, obviously, because the award as such enhanced her – though she may well have enhanced the award, funded, as it is, by conscience-money provided by the inventor of dynamite. After all, previous recipients were the Prime Minister of North Vietnam and Dr Kissinger; not exactly doves of peace, I should have thought. No, the glory of the award was precisely the glow of satisfaction it gave to all of us who love and respect Mother Teresa, in the knowledge that it would serve to spread yet further afield awareness of the ministry of love and compassion in which she and her Missionaries of Charity are so valiantly engaged.

When I first set eyes on her, which is now some fifteen years ago – the occasion a casual TV interview – I at once realized that I was in the presence of someone of unique quality. This was not due to her appearance, which is homely and unassuming, so that words like "charm" or "charisma" do not apply. Nor to her shrewdness and quick understanding, though these are very marked; nor even to her manifest piety and true humility and ready laughter. There is a phrase in one of the psalms that always, for me, evokes her presence: "the beauty of holiness" – that special beauty, amounting to a kind of pervasive luminosity generated by a life dedicated wholly to loving God and His creation. This, I imagine, is what the haloes in medieval paintings of saints were intended to convey.

Thinking about Mother Teresa, as I often do, and realizing that by all the odds she will one day be canonized, I try to sort out the various characteristics in her of a saint. First of all, contrary to what might be supposed, other-worldliness is not one of them. Mother Teresa is very firmly settled here on earth, in time and in mortality, and her judgements relating thereto have proved to be quite remarkably shrewd and perceptive. Her practicality never ceases to amaze me. Thus, she is now responsible for some two hundred and forty houses in different parts of the world, including some in places like the Yemen and Zagreb, which present particular hazards. The headquarters of a business of comparable size and distribution would occupy a whole skyscraper, filled with managerial staff, computers, secretaries, tape machines and teleprinters tapping away.

Mother Teresa manages without any of this plant and paraphernalia, dealing with her correspondence in her own hand, usually late at night, and travelling about the world in the most economical way possible. At one point she offered herself as an air hostess to Air India in return for free travel. Alas, the offer was not accepted, but what an air hostess she would have made! Money that comes in is exclusively for the poor, not for administration; in any case, she assumes, it will turn up as and when required. And so, miraculously, it does. She has even forbidden her co-workers to organize fund-raising campaigns, which, she insists, distract their attention from their true work of comforting and helping the lonely, the afflicted and the despairing.

On the one hand, she makes mystical concepts seem an integral part of day-to-day living; on the other, she, as it were, transcendentalizes our most ordinary conclusions and expectations. Thus, she persuades aspiring helpers who are too incapacitated to become active members of her order, that somehow or other their fortitude in accepting their affliction gives her additional strength and courage for her work; that their endurance of suffering is her powerhouse. I have myself seen a lady preparing to undergo her umpteenth operation all shining and joyful because she is convinced that thereby Mother Teresa will acquire extra muscle in the service of Christ. At the same time, she managed to induce high caste Indian ladies to minister to derelicts brought in from the streets of Calcutta – something that, as someone who has lived, one way and another, a number of years in India, I should never have believed possible.

Her response to happenings and circumstances is always so wonderfully apt. For instance, her response to her Peace Prize award was to disappear for a month into a strict retreat, leaving the cameramen and interviewers to disperse, the telephone calls, letters and telegrams unanswered. Or, while waiting to be interviewed on a coast-to-coast American TV talk show, and noting that advertisement after advertisement was of packaged food recommended as being non-fattening and non-nourishing, to remark, quietly but audibly: "I see that Christ is needed in television studios."

Of course, she enjoys the inestimable advantage of never looking at TV, listening to radio or reading the newspapers, and so has a clear notion of what is really going on in the world; the siren-voice of the consensus does not reach her. This enables her to post her Missionaries of Charity about the world so as to be exactly where they are most needed. Like St Francis with his friars, she expects them to carry laughter with them as well as charity; like an earlier St Theresa – of Avila, but Mother Teresa carefully explains that she is named after the little one, of Lisieux – in her standing orders, she does not overrate what this world has to offer.

The order she has founded is, I should suppose, as strict as any now in existence, if not stricter. Yet, although in orders that have softened the rigours of their rule, novices are few and far between, Mother Teresa's is bombarded by girls asking to enter. Some time ago she came to visit me with some twenty-five of these aspiring Missionaries of Charity, of numerous races and nations, and all, as it seemed to me, enchanting in their eagerness to join Mother Teresa, and their obvious delight at being accepted to share a life whose ardours contrast so sharply with the self-indulgence considered today to be synonymous with happiness and "quality of life". How curious that others seem not to understand, what is so clear to her, that the more that is asked on Christ's behalf, the more will be accorded, and vice versa!

I could go on and on enumerating the saintly qualities in Mother Teresa. Jean-Pierre de Caussade writes of how, all the time, the sequel to the New Testament is being written by saintly souls in the succession of the prophets and apostles, not in canonical books, but by continuing the history of divine purpose with their lives. So, just as great artists have painted the Incarnation, great writers described and dramatized it, great composers set it to music, great architects built it, great saints lived it, by Mother Teresa's mere presence, even just by thinking about her, the follies and confusions of our time are confuted, and once more God's Almighty Word leaps down from heaven, to live among us, full of grace and truth. This is what saints are for; you spell them out, and lo! the Holy Spirit has spoken.

One reason for my hesitating so long before becoming a Catholic was my disappointment at some of the human elements I saw in the Catholic Church. In spite of the following letter from Mother Teresa I still held back, and a number of years went by before I could make up my mind.

"I think, dear friend," she wrote, "I understand you better now. I am afraid I could not answer to your deep suffering. I don't know why, but you are to me like Nicodemus (who came to Jesus under cover of night), and I'm sure the answer is the same: 'Unless you become a little child . . .'

"I am sure you will understand beautifully everything – if you would only become a little child in God's hands. Your longing for God is so deep, and yet He keeps Himself away from you. He must be forcing Himself to do so, because He loves you so much as to give Jesus to die for you and for me. Christ is longing to be your Food. Surrounded with fullness of living Food, you allow yourself to starve.

"The personal love Christ has for you is infinite – the small difficulty you have regarding the Church is finite. Overcome the finite with the infinite. Christ has created you because He wanted you. I know what you feel – terrible longing, with dark emptiness – and yet He is the one in love with you. I do not know if you have seen these few lines before, but they fill and empty me:

> My God, my God, what is a heart
> That Thou should'st so eye and woo,
> Pouring upon it all Thy heart
> As if Thou had'st nothing else to do?

* * *

After all, the Church went on crusades, set up an inquisition, installed scandalous popes and countenanced monstrous iniquities. Institutionally speaking, these are perfectly comprehensible and even, in earthly terms, excusable. But in the mouthpiece of God on earth, belonging not just to history but to everlasting truth, they are not easily defended. Yet, as Hilaire Belloc truly remarked, the Church must be in God's hands because, seeing the people who have run it, it couldn't possibly have gone on existing if there weren't some help from above.

I also felt unable to take completely seriously, and therefore to believe in, the validity or permanence of any form of human authority. However, what goes on in one's mind and what goes on in one's soul aren't necessarily the same thing. There is something else, some other process going on inside one, to do with faith which is really more important and more powerful. I can no more explain conversion intellectually than I can explain why one falls in love with someone whom one marries. It's a very similar thing.

As far as Incarnation is concerned, I believe firmly in it. I believe that God did lean down to become Man in order that we could reach up to Him, and that the drama which embodies that Incarnation, the drama described in the Creed, took place. And I accept the drama as the key factor in the whole story. If you say to me, "Do you believe that Jesus's birth was by a virgin? Yes, I do, because I think the whole drama requires that. But that's entirely different from saying that I believe that a particular female, without anything else happening, conceived and bore a child and that that child was Jesus. In other words, I see it as an artistic truth rather than an historical truth. I think the Church began to destroy itself when it sought its evidence in historicity or in the process of science. The great truths the Church has enshrined through many centuries are artistic truths, which are much more truthful than any other kind of truth. The worst that could happen to the Christian religion would be to be provable in humanistic terms. It would be disastrous. For me, embracing Christianity is a question of faith not of rational proof, but at the same time a reasonable faith. Provided one accepts the initial jump of the Incarnation, everything else follows.

It was the Catholic Church's firm stand against contraception and abortion which finally made me decide to become a Catholic.

Contraception and abortion have made havoc both for the young and for the old. The terrible things that are going on, the precocious sexual practices of children, the debauchery in universities, making eroticism an end and not a means, are a consequence of violating the natural order of things. As the Romans treated eating as an end in itself, making themselves sick in a vomitorium so as to enable them to return to the table and stuff themselves with more delicacies, so people now end up in a sort of sexual vomitorium. The Church's stand is absolutely correct. It is to its eternal honour that it opposed contraception, even if the opposition failed. I think, historically, people will say it was a very gallant effort to prevent a moral disaster.

In spite of my awareness of the depth to which human beings can descend without God, I firmly believe that we are given the choice of Love or power. The way of Love is the way of the Cross, and it is only through the cross that we come to the Resurrection.

11

The Prospect of Death

The one sure thing about mortal existence is that it will end; the moment we are born, we begin to die. This basic fact of death is today highly unpalatable, to the point that extraordinary efforts are made, linguistically and in every other way, to keep death out of sight and mind.

Even those who for one reason or another advocate killing off unborn children and the debilitated old seek to clothe their murderous intentions in elusive terms; such as Retrospective Fertility Control for abortion, and Mercy Killing for euthanasia. A month spent in Florida in the company of fellow geriatrics gave me some idea of the lengths to which the old are induced to go in order to distract their thoughts from their impending demise. In, let us call it, Sunshine Haven, everything was done to make us feel that we were not really aged, but still full of youthful zest and expectations; if not teenagers, then keen-agers, perfectly capable of disporting ourselves on the dance floor, the beach, or even in bed. Withered bodies arrayed in dazzling summer wear, hollow eyes glaring out of garish caps, skulls plastered with cosmetics, lean shanks tanned a rich brown, bony buttocks encased in scarlet trousers – it all served to make a Florida beach on a distinct view a macabre version of Keats's Grecian Urn:

What men or gods are these? What maidens loath?
What mad pursuit? What struggle to escape?
What pipes and timbrels? What wild ecstasy?

Nearer at hand, the impression was more in the vein of Evelyn Waugh's *The Loved One*. At Forest Lawn, the original of Waugh's Whispering Glades, the cadavers are scented and anointed and dressed for their obsequies in their exotic best, down to underclothes; in Sunset Haven, pre-cadavers likewise array themselves for social occasions like young debutantes and their squires out on a spree, and behave accordingly, though sometimes with creaking joints and inward groans. Of all the amenities available in Sunset Haven – bingo, swimming pool, books, billiards and golf – the one never spoken of or advertised in any way is the crematorium, discreetly hidden away among trees and bushes, and unmentioned in the illustrated brochures. Yet evidently business is brisk through the winter months, despite the sunshine and the geriatric *joie de vivre* so much in evidence. Death becomes the dirty little secret that sex once was. Eros comes out of hiding, and old Father Time tries to secrete his scythe.

Another method of, as it were, keeping death under the carpet is to stow away the debilitated old in state institutions, where they live in a kind of limbo between life and death, heavily sedated and inert. Private institutions for the affluent old are naturally better equipped and staffed, but can be very desolating, too. Those under Christian auspices, especially when they are run by nuns, usually have long waiting lists, not so much because the prospective inmates are particularly pious, as because they want to be sure that some zealot for mercy killing will not finish them off arbitrarily by administering excessive sedation; or, if they happen to need to be in an iron lung or attached to a kidney machine, by pulling the plug, as it is put in today's rather disgusting medical jargon.

In any case, disposing of people who live inconveniently long, and of defectives of one sort and another, has, from the point of view of governments, the great advantage of saving money and personnel without raising a public hullabaloo – something governments are always on the look out for. It is, of course, inevitable that in a materialist society like ours death should seem terrible, and even inadmissible. If Man is the very apex of creation, with nothing greater than himself in the universe; if his earthly life exhausts the whole content of his existence, then, clearly, his definitive end, his death, is too outrageous to be contemplated, and so is better ignored.

Simone de Beauvoir, in her book *A Very Easy Death*, describes her mother's death from cancer as being "as violent and unforeseen as an engine stopping in the middle of the sky". The image is significant; death is seen, not as the finale of a drama; nor as the end of an act, to be followed by a change of scene and the rest of the play; not even as an animal expiring, but as the breakdown of a machine which suddenly and maddeningly stops working. "There is no such thing as a natural death", Madame de Beauvoir concludes. "All men must die, but for every man his death is an accident, and, even if he knows it and consents to it, an unjustifiable violation." In the light of such an attitude, death becomes a monstrous injustice, an act of brutal oppression, like, say the Vietnam War, or *apartheid* in South Africa. One imagines a demo led by Madame de Beauvoir, and all the demonstrators chanting in unison: "Death out! Death out! Death out!"

The slogan is not quite as preposterous as might at first glance be supposed; the crazy notion that some sort of drug might be developed which would make its takers immortal, a death pill to match the birth pill, has been seriously entertained. And how wonderfully ironical that *soma*, the drug in Aldous Huxley's *Brave New World* that was to make everyone happy for evermore, should have been the name originally chosen for thalidomide! Nor is it fanciful to detect in the mania for transplants of hearts, kidneys and other organs, perhaps even genitals, a hope that it may become possible to keep human beings going indefinitely, like vintage cars, by replacing their spare parts as they wear out.

Again, experimentation in the field of genetics would seem to hold out the prospect of being able in due course to produce forms of life not subject to death. Jonathan Swift, in *Gulliver's Travels*, showed a clearer sense of our true human condition when he made the immortal Stuldbrugs, encountered by Gulliver on his third voyage to the flying island of Laputa, not, as Gulliver had supposed they would be, wise, serene and knowledgeable, but rather the most miserable of creatures, excruciatingly boring to themselves and to others. Whenever they see a funeral Gulliver learns, they lament and repine that others are gone to a harbour of rest, at which they themselves never can hope to arrive.

Indeed, sanely regarded, death may be seen as an important factor in making life tolerable; I like very much the answer given by an octogenarian when asked how he accounted for his longevity – "Oh, just bad luck!" No doubt for this reason among others, death has often in the past been celebrated rather than abhorred; for instance, very exquisitely, by the Metaphysical Poets, among whom John Donne may be regarded as the very lauriate of death. So alluring did he find the prospect of dying that when he was Dean of St Paul's he had himself painted in his shroud so as to be reminded of the deliverance from life that lay ahead. Sleep, he points out, even just for a night, wonderfully refreshes us; how much more, then, will sleeping on into eternity be refreshing! And then:

> One short sleep past, we wake eternally,
> And Death shall be no more, Death thou shalt die.

In our own time, Dietrich Bonhoeffer manifested a similar attitude to death when, with his face shining in joyful expectation, he said to the two Nazi guards who had come to take him to be executed: "For you it is an end, for me a beginning." Likewise Blake when, on his deathbed, he told his wife Catherine that to him dying was no more than moving from one room to another. As his end approached he sang some particularly beautiful songs, which, he told Catherine, were not of his composition, but came directly from heaven.

Alas, I cannot claim total certainty of this order, and fall back on Pascal's famous wager, which requires us to bet on eternal survival or eternal extinction. Confronted with such a choice, as Pascal points out in his *Pensées*, the obvious course must be to back the former possibility, since then, "if you win, you win everything; if you lose, you lose nothing". So, I back eternal survival, knowing full well that if eternal extinction should be my lot, I shall never know that I have lost my bet, and taking no account of exotic notions like Reincarnation, or of the so-called "evidence" provided by people who have been in a coma and imagined they were dead. The fact is that to know what being dead is like, you have to die, just as to know what being born is like you have to be born.

I can say with truth that I have never, even in times of greatest preoccupation with carnal, worldly and egotistic pursuits, seriously doubted that our existence here is related in some mysterious way to a more comprehensive and lasting existence elsewhere; that somehow or other we belong to a larger scene than our earthly life provides, and to a wider reach of time than our earthly allotment of three score years and ten. Thus, death has seemed more alluring than terrible, even perhaps especially, as a belligerent of sorts in the 1939–45 war; for instance, wandering about in the London Blitz, and finding a kind of exaltation in the spectacle of a bonfire being made of old haunts like Fleet Street, Paternoster Row, the Inner Temple, as though, not only might I expect to die myself, but the world I knew, the way of life to which I belonged, was likewise fated to be extinguished. Now, death seems more alluring than ever, when, in the nature of things, it must come soon, and transmits intimations of its imminence by the aches and pains and breathlessness which accompany old age.

It has never been possible for me to persuade myself that the universe could have been created, and we, *homo sapiens*, so-called, have, generation after generation, somehow made our appearance to sojourn briefly on our tiny earth, solely in order to mount the interminable soap opera, with the same characters and situations endlessly recurring, that we call history. It would be like building a great stadium for a display of tiddly-winks, or a vast opera house for a mouth-organ recital.

There must, in other words, be another reason for our existence and that of the universe than just getting through the days of our life as best we may; some other destiny than merely using up such physical, intellectual and spiritual creativity as has been vouchsafed us. This, anyway, has been the strongly held conviction of the greatest artists, saints, philosophers and, until quite recent times, scientists, through the Christian centuries, who have all assumed that the New Testament promise of eternal life is valid, and that the great drama of the Incarnation which embodies it, is indeed the master drama of our existence. To suppose that these distinguished believers were all credulous fools whose folly and credulity in holding such beliefs has now been finally exposed, would seem to me to be untenable; and anyway I'd rather be wrong with Dante and Shakespeare and Milton, with Augustine of Hippo and Francis of Assisi, with Dr Johnson, Blake and Dostoevsky, than right with Voltaire, Rousseau, Darwin, the Huxleys, Herbert Spencer, H. G. Wells and Bernard Shaw.

It must be admitted that as the years pass – and how quickly they pass, their passing speeding up with the passage of time! – our world and living in it come to seem decidedly overrated. As Saint Theresa of Avila put it, no more than a night in a second-class hotel. Even so, it is extraordinary how even in old age, when ambition is an absurdity, lechery a bad joke, cupidity an irrelevance – how even then I find myself, as the General Confession in the Book of Common Prayer puts it so beautifully, following too much the devices and desires of my own heart. Talking to the young I have noticed with wry amusement how they assume that round the late sixties a kind of cut-off operates whereby the world, the flesh and the devil automatically lose their appeal. If only it were so!

The best I can hope for in my dotage is to emulate the state of mind of the Sage in Dr Johnson's *Rasselas*, reflecting that of his creator:

> My retrospect of life recalls to my view many opportunities of good neglected, much time squandered upon trifles and more lost in idleness and vacancy. I leave many great designs unattempted, and many great attempts unfinished. My mind is burdened with no heavy crime, and therefore I compose myself to tranquillity; endeavour to abstract my thoughts from hopes and cares which, though reason knows them to be vain, still keep their old possession of the heart; expect with serene humility, that hour which nature cannot long delay; and hope to possess in a better state, that happiness which here I could not find, and that virtue which here I have not attained.

None the less, the mystery remains; and ever must. Some eight decades ago I came into the world, full of cries and wind and hiccups; now I prepare to leave it, also full of cries and wind and hiccups. Whence I came I cannot know, least of all in the light of contemporary myths like Darwinian evolution, Freudian psychology, situational ethics, Marxist prophecy, and so on – surely the most absurd ever. Whither I go, if anywhere, I can only surmise helped thereto by the testimony of true visionaries like the author of *The Cloud of Unknowing*, Blake, Dostoevsky, and, of course, above all Jesus Christ. By inspired works of art like Chartres Cathedral and the *Missa Solemnis*, by the dedicated lives of saints and mystics; above all, by the Incarnation and all its consequences, in history, in what we still call Western Civilization, now toppling into its final collapse, in providing infallible signposts in the quest for God.

The hardest thing of all to explain is that death's nearness in some mysterious way makes what is being left behind – I mean our earth itself, its shapes and smells and colours and creatures, all that one has known and loved and lived with – the more entrancing; as the end of a bright June day somehow encapsulates all the beauty of the daylight hours now drawing to a close; or as the last notes of a Beethoven symphony manage to convey the splendour of the whole piece. Checking out of St Theresa of Avila's second-class hotel, as the revolving doors take one into the street outside, one casts a backward look at the old place, overcome with affection for it, almost to the point of tears.

So, like a prisoner awaiting his release, like a schoolboy when the end of term is near, like a migrant bird ready to fly south, like a patient in hospital anxiously scanning the doctor's face to see whether a discharge may be expected, I long to be gone. Extricating myself from the flesh I have too long inhabited, hearing the key turn in the lock of Time so that the great doors of Eternity swing open, disengaging my tired mind from its interminable conundrums and my tired ego from its wearisome insistencies. Such is the prospect of death.

I am eighty-four years old, an octogenarian who has done much that he ought not to have done and left undone much that he ought to have done, and lived fourteen years longer than the three score years and ten which, the Bible tells, will be but labour and sorrow, they pass away so soon.

For me, intimations of immortality, deafness, failing eyesight, loss of memory, the afflictions of old age, release me from preoccupation with worldly fantasy and free me to meditate on spiritual reality, to recall Archbishop Fulton Sheen's remark that Christendom is over but not Christ.

And so I live, just for each day, knowing my life will soon be over, and that I, like Michelangelo at the end of his life ". . . have loved my friends and family. I have loved God and all His creation. I have loved life and now I love death as its natural termination . . ."*, knowing that although Christendom may be over – Christ lives!

---

* From *"The Agony and the Ecstasy"* by Irving Stone

Acknowledgements

In the course of my dialogue with Robert Nowell, published in *St Anthony's Messenger* on the occasion of my reception into the Catholic Church, I have described my reasons for my decision to become a Catholic in my replies to his searching questions.